J. A Van Aalst

Chinese Music

J. A Van Aalst

Chinese Music

ISBN/EAN: 9783337087128

Printed in Europe, USA, Canada, Australia, Japan

Cover: Foto ©Thomas Meinert / pixelio.de

More available books at **www.hansebooks.com**

THE HALL OF CLASSICS, WHERE CEREMONIES ARE OCCASIONALLY PERFORMED

CHINA.

IMPERIAL MARITIME CUSTOMS.

II.—SPECIAL SERIES: No. 6.

CHINESE MUSIC.

BY

J. A. VAN AALST

(Chinese Imperial Customs Service).

PUBLISHED BY ORDER OF

𝕿𝖍𝖊 𝕴𝖓𝖘𝖕𝖊𝖈𝖙𝖔𝖗 𝕲𝖊𝖓𝖊𝖗𝖆𝖑 𝖔𝖋 𝕮𝖚𝖘𝖙𝖔𝖒𝖘.

SHANGHAI:
PUBLISHED AT THE STATISTICAL DEPARTMENT OF THE INSPECTORATE GENERAL OF CUSTOMS.
AND SOLD BY
MESSRS. KELLY & WALSH, SHANGHAI, YOKOHAMA, AND HONGKONG.
LONDON: P. S. KING & SON, CANADA BUILDING, KING STREET, WESTMINSTER, S.W.
1884.

INTRODUCTION.

THE Chinese have the reputation of being a strange people, with a peculiar language, peculiar institutions, customs, and manners, utterly different from those of our Western countries.

Since Chinese ports were thrown open to foreigners, the influx of visitors of all kinds has continually increased. Missionaries, diplomats, travellers—some led there by duty, others attracted by the prospect of a new field for studies, and others guided by mere curiosity—have crossed the country in all directions. From these visits has resulted a large number of books—relations of travels, descriptions of country, customs, and manners—books on any subject, all tending to acquaint Western nations with the wonderful Celestial Empire, and, principally, to point out the immense difference existing between Chinese and European ideas.

Amongst the subjects which have been treated with the least success by foreign writers, Chinese Music ranks prominently. If mentioned at all in their books, it is simply to remark that "it is detestable, noisy, monotonous; that it hopelessly outrages our Western notions of music," etc. I do not wish to create any discussions by contradicting these and many other erroneous statements found in descriptions of Chinese Music: it would take too long a time.

In the description I give here I will endeavour to point out the contrasts or similarity between Western and Chinese Music, to present abstruse theories in the least tiresome way, to add details never before published, and to give a short yet concise account of Chinese Music.

I am not pretentious enough to think that my work will be utterly irreproachable. Mistakes are so easily made; and if I have just alluded to the many mistakes which are found in books, it is merely with the intention of showing how careful we must be when writing, and, much more, how indulgent we need be towards the writings of others.

I should deem it unfair not to mention that Mr. HIPPISLEY, one of our Commissioners of Customs, is entitled to my most sincere gratitude for his kindness in reading the manuscript and correcting the many faults which ordinarily slip from one's pen when attempting to write in any but one's own language.

J. A. VAN AALST.

CHINESE MUSIC.

ON ANCIENT MUSIC.

THE origin of music may from its nature be attributed to times coeval with the appearance of man on earth. Indeed, what is music? Listen to the accents of Nature! Hear the murmur of streams, the whisper of trees' leaves, the moaning of winds, the distant rolling of thunder, the resounding majesty of the ocean! Notice the bleating of the timid sheep, the lowing of herds, the singing of the lark, the animated cadence of the nightingale! What are all those voices but music, but a concert—a hymn which impresses the soul and elevates it to the ideal of infinite beauty?

When man began to contemplate the vast universe, his attention was naturally directed to harmonious Nature. The singing of birds, above all, must have deeply impressed him and led him to vocal imitation. In the course of time he contrived to combine the natural sounds of his voice into a system, to arrange them into melodies agreeable to the ear, and, finally, to make instruments by which the melodies could be rendered.

Mythology shows us ORPHEUS, on the Thracian mountains, submitting the forest monsters to the power of his lyre; ARION escaping submersion; AMPHION building cities. If we open the annals of history we find FU HSI playing on the *ch'in*; TIMOTHEUS subjugating ALEXANDER; the rustic Spartans proscribing every art except music; the same Spartans, often defeated, led to victory by the songs of the Athenian TYRTÆUS. In the Holy Scriptures we are told of TUBAL CAIN, the sixth descendant from CAIN, manufacturing instruments; of MOSES singing a hymn with accompaniment of timbrels, after the passage of the Red Sea; and of King DAVID playing on the harp. The Egyptian history mentions PTOLEMY PHILADELPHUS employing a band of 600 musicians to celebrate the feast of Bacchus; and PTOLEMY AULETES, or the flute-player, competing in his own palace with the greatest professional musicians.

Indeed, no nation on earth has existed that did not love that enchanting art, however rude and artless the primitive systems may have been. It is everywhere an instinct of Nature, a want of the soul; it is found in the camps, in the forests, in the gilded palaces of the despots of the East, in the meadows of America; it cheers solitude; it charms society; it animates at the same time war and pastoral life.

The Greeks, the Chinese, and all the ancient nations speak of the mysterious influence of music; and still their systems, if compared with ours, were only imperfect embryos. But it cannot be denied that the national music of every country, however simple it may be, has a mystic influence on the passions of its inhabitants; some airs are principally capable of raising or depressing the spirits, of causing an electrical commotion in the hearts of the auditors.

Great discussions have arisen on the subject of Ancient Music, but, in spite of many learned researches, commentaries, and theories, we cannot boast of knowing much about it; and many a brave man is still racking his brains, and will succumb before having resolved the question and having learned more on the subject than what has been handed down to us by PTOLEMÆUS, PLUTARCH, and PLATO.

From what we know of Greek music we can infer that it was simply a system for regulating the movements of dances, pantomimes, and poetry; so the mysterious influence spoken of may have been due more to the words and gestures than to the sounds themselves. The Greeks had several gamuts with an irregular distribution of intervals. Of those gamuts, some were used for music of a solemn character; some were adapted to merry, lively, martial music; and some others to music of a soft and pathetic character. As for the notation, the alphabetical letters alone were used; harmony, modulation, and even melody (as we understand it) were unknown. Their music was divided into three principal kinds: the ἁρμόνια, or church music; the σίκιννις, for grotesque occasions; and the κόρδαξ, for dancing. All this is equally applicable to Chinese music, as will be shown hereafter.

Music is in principle romantic and fanciful, and therefore it is closely related to religion. Everywhere where polytheism or idolatry has existed we find music occupying only a subordinate position, the highest rank being given to the plastic art—to sculpture; whereas among the nations whose worship was of a more spiritual character we find music occupying the first place. Indeed, the Hebrews, although often tainted with idolatry, possessed the most advanced system of their time; and the Chinese worshippers of Shang-ti have a kind of music unknown to the adherents of Buddha and Tao. On the other hand, the uncivilised, idolatrous nations have scarcely any musical system.

It is an uncontested fact that music has gradually risen and progressed with Christianity. Through its character of ineffable spiritualism, the art of sounds alone was able to render the Christian idea of an uncreated God. Antiquity appealed to the plastic arts for representations of its gods, because those gods never ceased to affect the forms and passions of humanity; but a religion of abnegation and mystic contemplation required as interpreter an art whose aspiration is unbounded, whose element is impalpable, as music.

During the first three centuries of our era, when Christians were exposed to persecutions and had to conceal themselves to pray, music had of course but little place in worship; but in the 4th century, when Christian perseverance had overpowered the cruel paganism, AMBROSIUS, archbishop of Milan, adopted four of the Greek gamuts for the liturgical music of the church.

Some additions to the number of scales were made by Pope GREGORY during the 6th century; but the greatest improvements, principally the system of notation on a stave, are due to GUIDO D'AREZZO, a Benedictine monk of the 11th century.

It was only during the 13th century that harmonic chords first came into use; until then singing was all in unison. But the most important revolution in modern music was effected during the last years of the 17th century, when the two great divisions, major and minor, were introduced. Since then our system has continually progressed, and all the mysteries of the world of sounds have been brought to light.

Our present complicated system of music is thus comparatively modern.

If ancient music exercised a magic influence on its hearers, what shall we say of our modern art which elevates its admirers to the highest pitch of idealism to which imagination can be brought; whose romance transports us out of our spheres, out of the limited circle of our knowledge; whose accents make us shed tears when the subject is sad, tremble when it is terrible, love when it is tender, admire when it is great, adore when it is divine? This accounts for the irresistible attraction exercised by music on those feminine, weak, timid natures, which a continual musing elevates above the tribulations of this world. Woman, endowed with the most exquisite feeling of sensitiveness, loves music with passion, because, like her, it softens the manners, disarms force by grace, brings nearer and binds together the different elements of society.

It also accounts for the instinctive aversion felt by those positive minds, those unbelievers, who consider music as an organised row, a kind of noise submitted to the most delirious rules and expressed by means of an artillery of instruments called pianos, trombones, cornets, etc., which, they say, are best adapted to drive one mad or to make one appreciate surdity.

Fortunately for the fine arts, this unfeeling part of mankind is by far the smallest, and their indifference hardly affects the enthusiasm of others.

PLATO says that music affected considerably the constitution of the State; CONFUCIUS was of the same opinion. Indeed, all skilful politicians, all wise rulers, are aware that they must not look upon their subjects as abstractions, moving them about like the pawns on a chess-board, without considering that men have senses; that these senses create passions; that the science of governing men is simply the science of guiding their feelings; that the basis of all human institutions rests on public and private customs; and that the fine arts are essentially of a moral character, since they render the man who cultivates them better and happier. And what is health but the essence of happiness, the result of internal contentment, the peaceful feelings of the soul manifested on the exterior envelope of man.

This dissertation may seem out of place in an article on Chinese music. Nevertheless it is a fact that the Chinese have had the very same ideas; and this consideration, taken in connexion with several astonishing similarities between all the ancient systems, will re-enforce the belief of music's common origin.

ON CHINESE MUSIC.

Music in China has undoubtedly been known since the remotest antiquity. It is said to have been invented by the Emperor Fu Hsi (B.C. 2852); but the invention of music can scarcely be attributed to anybody. The revelation of it must have proceeded from man's admiration of Nature. It is, say the Chinese, the essence of the harmony existing between heaven, earth, and man; and since we believe that all human beings come forth from Adam and subsequently from Noah, we may reasonably infer that the chiefs of each of the great families carried with them the principles of the then existing music: these principles, differently influenced by the more or less artistic skill of the different nations, have formed the various systems, which at first seem diametrically opposed, but which, when compared and deprived of their special and characteristic individuality, show such coincidence, such striking similarities as to render their common origin indubitable.

The first invaders of China[1] certainly brought with them certain notions of music. The aborigines themselves[2] had also some kind of musical system, which their conquerors admired and probably mixed with their own.

We read in the 通典 (*Tung-tien*) that the music of the Emperor Fu Hsi was called 扶來 (*fu-lai*) or 立本 (*li-p'u*); that of the Emperor Shên Nung, 扶特 (*fu-tê*) or 下謀 (*hsia-mou*); and that of the Emperor Huang Ti, 咸池 (*hsien-chih*), or the "all-pervading influence."[3] What the real meaning of these names was is not known, and they may be compared to the obscure musical terms of the Bible. At that time music was not regulated by any laws; each Emperor had his own system, and they did not always agree.[4] Beginning with Huang Ti, "the Yellow Emperor" (B.C. 2697), Chinese music assumes its characteristic form. A certain note is taken as the base; sounds are fixed, and receive names; comparisons are drawn between the notes and the celestial bodies; music becomes a necessity in the State—a key to good government. Huang Ti hears it.[5] To obey the desire of his human nature, he renders it manifest through all the Empire to comply with the wishes of heaven; he practises it, to be in accordance with the rites of propriety; and he establishes it in the Empire, to render the people better and happier. The succeeding Emperors followed the system of Huang Ti, and composed hymns: the great Shun (B.C. 2255) composed the piece called *Ta Shao*, the very same which, 1,600 years later, so deeply impressed Confucius that for three months "he did not know the taste of meat,"—that is, he was so captured by the beauty of the piece that for three months he thought of nothing else. All the philosophers are unanimous in their praise of ancient music:

[1] They were a band of immigrants fighting their way amongst the aborigines, and supposed to have come from the south of the Caspian Sea.

[2] The *Li*, the *Kiao*, and the *Yao* tribes, remnants of which are said to be still in existence in South China.

[3] The 通典 (*Tung-tien*), or "Complete Dictionary," by 杜佑 (Tu Yu), says: 伏羲樂名扶來亦曰立本. 神農樂名扶特亦曰下謀. 黃帝作咸池.

[4] See Preface to the 闕里芭志, which says: 五帝不和合樂由來尙矣

[5] See 韓苑洛志樂, chapter 13: 吾奏之以人徵之以天行之以禮義建之以大淸.

See 莊子, which says: 子在齊聞韶三月不知肉味.

it was eminently sweet and harmonious, and produced inexpressible sensations of pleasure in the hearers. Therefore they lament and regret that it has been lost.[1]

It is most probable that the merits of ancient music consisted chiefly, like that of the Greeks, in regulating the movements of dances and poetry. Indeed, the Chinese idea is that music without poetry is no music at all.[2]

Music, says the *Musical Recorder*, proceeds from the heart of man.[3] The harmony of the heart produces the harmony of the breath, the harmony of the breath produces that of the voice, and the voice is the emblem of the harmony existing between heaven and earth.[4]

According to Chinese ideas, music rests on two fundamental principles—the 神理 (*shin-li*), or spiritual, immaterial principle, and the 器數 (*ch'i-sha*), or substantial form. All natural productions are represented by unity; all that requires perfecting at the hands of man is classed under the generic term 萬 (*wan*), plurality. Unity is above, it is heaven; plurality is below, it is earth. The immaterial principle is above, that is, it is inherent in material bodies, and is considered their 本 (*pên*), basis, origin. The material principle is below; it is the 形 (*hsing*), form or figure of the *shin-li*. The form is limited to its proper shape by 數 (*shu*), number, and it is subjected to the rule of the *shin-li*. Therefore when the material principle of music (that is, the instruments) is clearly and rightly illustrated, the corresponding spiritual principle (that is, the essence, the sounds of music) becomes perfectly manifest, and the State's affairs are successfully conducted.

If all this seems obscure, the fault lies with the Chinese.

Of all the ancient music nothing remains except the above abstruse theories. The Emperor She Huang-ti (B.C. 246), the destroyer of books, came; he ordered the annihilation of all books, with the exception of works on medicine, agriculture, and divination. The decree was obeyed as faithfully as possible by an uneducated soldiery, who made it the pretext of domiciliary visits, exactions, and pitiless destruction. Music-books and instruments shared the same fate as every object which could give rise to any remembrance of past times,[5] and a long night of ignorance rested on the country, to such an extent that "at the rise of the Han dynasty the great music-master, Chi, whose ancestors had for generations held the same dignity, scarcely remembered anything about music but the noise of tinkling bells and dancers' drums."

Under the subsequent dynasties great efforts were made to revive music. Ancient books and instruments were discovered in the places where they had been concealed at the time of the destruction of books, new books were written, instruments made, but the frequent political changes to which this country has been subject since the beginning of our era has not allowed

[1] 嘅古樂論亡.
[2] 樂無詩非樂也.
[3] *See* 樂記. chapter 17 of *Li-chi*: 凡音之起由人心生也.
[4] 心和則氣和氣和則聲和聲和故天地之和.
[5] 秦火古樂失傳.
[6] 漢興樂家有制氏以雅樂聲律世世在大樂官但能紀其鏗鏘鼓舞而不能言其義

of much time being devoted to music. Moreover, the authors who then wrote on the subject of music do not agree in their theories, and their successors have confused the different systems. During the present dynasty the Emperors K'ANG HSI and CH'IEN LUNG have done much to bring music back to its old splendour, but their efforts cannot be said to have been very successful. A total change has taken place in the ideas of that people which has been everywhere represented as unchangeable; they have changed, and so radically that the musical art, which formerly always occupied the place of honour, is now deemed the lowest calling a man can profess. There is still in Peking a Board of Music connected with the Board of Rites (just as the Romans had a college of flute-players), but the officers seem little anxious to distinguish themselves.

Serious music, which according to the classics is considered a necessary complement of education, is totally abandoned. Very few Chinese are able to play on the *ch'in*, the *sh'ing*, or the *yin-lo*, and still fewer are acquainted with the theory of the *lüs*.

Chinese music must be divided into two different kinds: ritual or sacred music, which is passably sweet, and generally of a minor character; and the theatrical or popular music. The populace, as every foreigner in China has experienced, delights in the deafening noise of the gong, accompanied by the shrieking tones of the clarionet; and such music requires no scientific study. Who has not met a funeral or a wedding procession where four or five clarionet-players blow their souls out with furious accompaniment of drums and gongs? Let it not be thought that the present Chinese do not like music. They do everything in music: they are born, they worship, they marry, and they die in music. Only they do not find it dignified to perform it themselves, not even as "amateurs." The streets are continually paraded by bands of two, three, or four musicians, mostly blind men, who go from gate to gate offering their services.

Western music is not at all appreciated in China. The Chinaman seems to pity us for being still so far back in this particular line when we have shown our superiority in all other branches of science. It may be very patriotic for the Chinese to have the best opinion possible of their own music, but it will not prevent foreigners finding it monotonous, noisy, and disagreeable.

ON THE LÜS.

The *lüs* (律 呂) are a series of bamboo tubes, the longest of which measures 9 inches, and which are supposed to render the 12 chromatic semitones of the octave.

The discovery of the *lüs* is somewhat fabulous. HUANG TI is reputed to be the inventor: he arranged them according to the *pa-kua*,[1] or mysterious symbols of FU HSI. HUANG TI sent one of his ministers, LANG LUN, to a place called Tahsia (which has been identified with Bactria, the mother of cities, from its unrivalled antiquity and splendour), situated west of

---

[1] The 八卦 (*pa-kua*) are eight diagrams drawn by the Emperor FU HSI, and which are used by the Chinese who believe that they represent the manifold changes which take place in Nature and in the affairs of the world) for purposes of divination. Chaos, or primitive existence, is unity: ———. One divided becomes two: —— ——. From these figures, one whole line and one divided, placed above each other (——— ——— ——— ——— etc.) the eight diagrams were formed. *(See* Montigny's book, " A View of China," etc., p. 118.)

黄帝制律呂與伏羲畫卦

the Kuénlun Mountains (the Olympus of China and the supposed source of the *fêng-shui*), to procure bamboo tubes to make the *lüs*. It appears that there is a valley there called Chiehku, where bamboos of regular thickness grow. LING LUN cut the piece of bamboo which is between two knots, and the sound emitted by this tube he considered as the base, the pitch-key, the tonic.[1] He arranged a series of 12 tubes, according to the ideas of his master, and they received the name 律 呂 *(lüs)*—that is, laws, principles, pitch-pipes.

Now, what led the inventor to the division of the octave into twelve semitones, each represented by one *lü?* Several versions are given :—

1°. Some say that he arrived at it by listening to the singing of the Fêngs or Fêngs (a powerful tribe living south of the Yangtze-kiang), the voices of the men giving him six demitones and those of the women the remaining six.[?]

2°. Others give the same theory with this particular change, that the Fêngs were not human beings, but birds ; the male being called 鳳 *(fêng)*, and the female 凰 *(hwang)*.[3] Unfortunately for this theory, a third account assures us that these birds were simply imaginary.[4]

3°. Another writer attributes to the rolling waves of the Yellow River the idea of the first sound. The bamboos growing on its borders were used to render it.[5]

4°. Another writer, less poetical but not less positive, is convinced that LING LUN cut his bamboos according to the terms of a triple progression of 12 numbers, as 1, 3, 9, 27, 81, etc., which, indeed, exhibit the numerical values of a series of perfect fifths.[6]

But without questioning to what extent these theories may be acceptable, it is more reasonable to believe that the discovery of the 12 divisions of the octave was due to simple and natural causes.

That the ancient Chinese should notice the difference of pitch between the sounds emitted by tubes of different length is quite natural ; that they contrived to find a tube the sound of which corresponded exactly to the fundamental note of the then existing music is not astonishing ; that they then became anxious to have tubes corresponding to the other sounds of their scale is quite comprehensible ; and that when comparing, blowing, or cutting they discovered the way to the division of the octave into 12 semitones is not at all impossible.

The Chinese have always been fond of seeking the similitude or contrasts existing between everything in creation. Between heaven and earth, they say, there is perfect harmony. Now, 3 is the emblem of heaven, 2 is the symbol of earth.[7] If two sounds are in the proportion of 3 to 2, they will harmonise as perfectly as heaven and earth. On this principle a second tube was cut, measuring exactly two-thirds of the length of the first tube, and the

[1] 黃帝使伶倫自大夏之西昆崙之陰取竹之嶰谷生其竅厚均者斷兩節間而吹之以爲黃鐘之宮.
[2] DOUGLAS' "China," p. 162.
[3] "Journal of the North-China Branch of the Royal Asiatic Society," No. VIII, 1874, p. 96.
[4] Morrison's Dictionary ; character 凰.
[5] Amiot, "Mémoires sur les Chinois."
[6] Paul Perny's Dictionary, Part II.
[7] The 漢志 says : 參天兩地.

sound rendered was the perfect fifth, which in our Western music is also expressed by the ratio of 3 to 2.

The second bamboo being treated on the same principle, produced a third tube measuring exactly two-thirds of the length, and giving a note a perfect fifth higher than that of the second tube. This new sound seeming too far distant from the first or fundamental note, the length of the producing tube was doubled (that is, four-thirds of the second tube's whole length was taken instead of two-thirds), and the note became an octave lower.

All the tubes were cut on the same principle; the relation of 3 to 2 representing the harmony existing between heaven and earth. They engendered one another and always measured two-thirds or four-thirds of the whole length of their generator. The *lüs* were therefore divided into two classes, the 陽律 *(yong lüs)* and the 陰呂 *(yin lüs)*, or males and females, positives and negatives, perfect and imperfect.

According to the 易經 *(I King)*, chaos was divided into two parts, *yong* answering to male energy, and *yin* corresponding to the female principle. All that is strong and superior is *yong*; *yin* indicates dependence, inferiority. Everything in Nature belongs to one of these two grand categories, from whose combinations and reciprocal action results all that exists or takes place in the universe. The *lüs* 1, 3, 5, 7, 9, and 11 were considered as *yong*; the even numbers were classed as *yin*; but it is well to remark that these distinctions did not at all affect the tones, and were made simply to please the Chinese ideas of the time. Other comparisons were drawn between the 12 *lüs*, the 12 moons, the 12 Chinese hours, etc.

The first tube, which was considered as the basis, the generator of all the others, received the name 黃鐘 *(hoang-chong)*. The sound produced by it was named 宮 *(kong)*, and became the tonic or key-note of a kind of semi-diatonic scale of 12 degrees, nearly *identical* with our chromatic gamut, the only difference being that our scale is *tempered*, while that of the Chinese is left untouched.

Temperament denotes a small, and to the ear almost imperceptible, deviation from the absolute purity of intervals which compose our scale. It is well known that 12 perfect fifths employed within the space of an octave (like the 12 Chinese sounds) exceed the ratio of the octave, or that of 2 to 1, by the *ditonic comma*, a small interval expressed by the ratio of 531,441 to 524,288. Our ear is so constructed that it cannot endure the excess or deficiency of a whole *comma* in any interval without being offended, and therefore it has been found expedient to diminish each fifth by one-twelfth of the *ditonic comma*, instead of diminishing only one fifth by the entire *comma*.

That is what we call *temperament* in Western music, and it is the absence of it that causes some of the Chinese intervals to appear to us either too high or too flat. We will prove mathematically the difference when speaking of the diatonic scale.

The following diagram will illustrate the *lüs*, giving their names, the moons, hours, etc., to which they correspond, the musical sounds they emit (supposing *hoang-hang* to give our C), their corresponding notes in our music, etc.

The *lüs* follow each other at the interval of half a tone.

三 分 損 益 上 下 和 生
配 五 行 四 時 八 卦 四 隔 十 二 辰

No. 3.

DIAGRAM SHOWING HOW THE LÜS GENERATE ONE ANOTHER

The question has been raised as to whether the *lü* were open at both ends or not. Those acquainted with the theory of the vibration of tubes will readily admit that they were stopped at one end, for the following reasons.

Sound in a tube, open or not, is produced by the vibrating movement of the air, and the sound will vary in pitch according to the degree of pressure of the air. The different notes so produced are called *harmonics*. The longer and narrower the tube, the more harmonics it will give.

A long tube open at both ends will give the following harmonics, which are marked 1, 2, 3, etc., according to their place in the succession of sounds.

A tube closed at one end will give only the harmonics marked with odd numbers, with this important peculiarity, that to produce the same note this tube requires only half the length of an open tube.

The first *huang-chung* tube measured only 1 foot. An open tube of that size would scarcely give any sound, whereas a corked tube 1 foot long gives the same note as an open tube 2 feet long. Moreover, the tubes of the Pandean pipe, which was a collection of bamboos made on the principle of the *lü*, were closed at the lower end.

To their series of 12 *lü* the Chinese added two new series, one lower and one higher. The *lü* were used merely to regulate the instruments and give a uniform pitch to the music. The diameter of all the *lü* must be the same.[1] MÊNG K'ANG (孟 康) says that the circumference of all tubes diminishes according to their length, but this is explicitly contradicted by TS'AI TZŬ (蔡子), who quotes CHÊNG K'ANG-CH'ÊNG (鄭康成) and TS'AI YUNG (蔡邕) (two great wine-bibbers and famous writers on music), and he flatly declares that MÊNG K'ANG and his adherents know nothing about music.[2] The tubes were all of the same thickness, circumference, and diameter; only the length varied according to the sounds. *Huang-chung*, or the first tube, was 1 foot in length in reality, but that foot was considered as being only 9 inches, because 9 is perfectly divisible by 3, whereas 10 is not.[3]

[1] 鄭康成月令註, which says: 凡律空圍九分 徑三分.
[2] 蔡子：康昭等不通律呂
此黄鐘之體數也 十分 將用之 九 以 丐 十.

When the *lüs* were first invented they were well-selected bamboos, but in subsequent times, principally during the Chin (晉) dynasty, the *lüs* were made of copper, of marble, and of jadestone. The opinion was that they would thus be less subject to atmospheric changes.

In order to illustrate fully the difference between the 12 *lüs* and the 12 semitones of our chromatic scale (tempered form), I give here a table showing the names of our notes corresponding to the Chinese *lüs*, the length of each *lü* in Chinese inches, according to the best and most reliable Chinese critics[1]; and the same length reduced to 120th parts of an inch and compared with the numerical values of our notes.

One Chinese foot is equal to 0.255 mètres, and our C is supposed to be *huang-chung*.

COMPARATIVE TABLE OF CHINESE AND WESTERN NOTES.

NAMES OF LÜS.	Corresponding Western Notes.	Length of Lüs in Chinese Inches.	Length of Lüs reduced to 120th Parts of an Inch.	Required Length of Tubes to render corresponding Western Notes.
Huang-chung, upper	C	4.3853	526.237	540
Ying-chung	B	4.66	559.2	576
Wu-i	B♭	4.8848	586.176	607.5
Nan-lu	A	5.3	636	645.3
I-tse	A♭	5.551	666.12	683.1
Lin-chung	G	6	720	720
Jui-pin	G♭	6.28	753.6	768.45
Chung-lu	F	6.5824	789.888	810
Ku-shi	E	7.1	852	864
Chia-chung	E♭	7.4373	892.476	910.71
Tai-tsu	D	8	960	963.99
Ta-lu	D♭	8.376	1005.12	1024.578
Huang-chung, base	C	9	1080	1080

By the above table it is seen that while the base and the fifth perfectly agree, all the other notes of the Chinese scale are too sharp, and consequently could not possibly be rendered on our Western tempered instruments. Besides, the octave is so high as to be very unpleasing to our Western ears. This is the principal reason why Chinese music does not leave a better impression on the minds of foreigners.

[1] 轉苑洛直解, 楊忠愍志樂, 胡安定律呂議, 鄭埰成月介註, 蔡邕銅龠銘, 班固漢前志, 司馬遷律書, 司馬貞索隱, 程奠考, and others.

OF THE PITCH.

What was the real pitch of the first *hwang-chung* tube?

The size, capacity, and material of the tubes have so often been changed during the successive dynasties that it has become almost impossible to form any acceptable conclusion on this subject.

Père Amiot, who died more than a century ago, gives F as the equivalent of *hwang-chung*; but he says himself in his works that he adopted this key because the strains of his harmonium impressed his Chinese hearers much more when he was playing in the key of F than when he played in any other key.

The present pitch approaches our D (601½ vibrations per second) as nearly as possible. The principal fixed instruments, as the *gin-lo*, the *sheng*, the flute, all give the D as *tonic*. But, with the view of pointing out in the clearest manner the similarity or contrast of Chinese music to our Western music, I have thought it convenient to give our C as the equivalent of *hwang-chung*, and to have our natural scale of C in apposition to the Chinese natural scale.

CHINESE SYSTEM OF NOTATION.

The 12 lüs, as has been shown before, formed a kind of semi-diatonic scale, resembling more or less our Western chromatic gamut. The ancient Chinese might thus have had hepta tonic and chromatic scales in all the keys; they did not, however, extend the use of their discovery so far, for up to the time of the Yin (殷) dynasty (B.C. 1300), only five notes—the sounds emitted by the five first lüs (see Diagram No. 2)—were in general use.[1]

To express these five sounds in writing, certain characters had been selected; they were—

宮 *(kung)*.
商 *(shang)*.
角 *(chiao)*.
徵 *(chih)*.
羽 *(yü)*.

But at the beginning of the Chou (周) dynasty (B.C. 1100) two more notes (the sounds emitted by lüs Nos. 6 and 7 of Diagram No. 2) were introduced.[2]

These were called—

變宮 *(pien-kung)*, literally changing into *kung*; and
變徵 *(pien-chih)*,   ..   *chih*.

Tsai Tzi (蔡 子) says: "Between *kung* and *shang*, *shang* and *chiao*, *chih* and *yü*, there is only the interval of one *lü*; we skip over one *lü* and use the next one (see Diagram No. 1); but between *chiao* and *chih*, *yü* and *kung*, there is an interval of two *lüs*. Now, when the notes are separated only by one *lü* the distance is not great, and their succession is satisfactory; but when two *lüs* stand between two notes the connexion between these seems interrupted."[3] To remedy this deficiency, the two *pien* were added to the scale, bringing the number of notes to seven; and these were called the seven principles, because they are produced by the first seven tubes, and because, as seen in Diagram No. 2, they engender one another.

The ancient scale was therefore as follows. Like the European diatonic scale, it is composed of five full tones and two half tones; but one of the half tones is found in the Chinese gamut between the fourth and fifth degrees, whereas in the Western gamut it stands between the third and fourth degrees.

自殷以前但有五音

自周以來加二聲謂之七聲. etc.

宮與商. 商與角. 徵與羽. 相去皆一律. 角與徵. 羽與宮. 相去隔二律. 一各
則近而加. 二律則遠而不相及. 故. etc.

Names of Notes.		Law by which the Notes are produced.		Western equivalent Notes.
Kung	宮	Hoang-chung	黃鐘	C
Shang	商	Tae-tsu	太簇	D
Kio	角	Ku-hsi	姑洗	E
Pien-chih	變徵	Jui-pin	蕤賓	F♯
Chih	徵	Lin-chung	林鐘	G
Yu	羽	Nan-lu	南呂	A
Pien-kung	變宮	Ying-chung	應鐘	B
Kung	宮	Hoang-chung	黃鐘	C

This scale remained in use unchanged until the rise of the Yüan (元) dynasty (14th century), the founder of which was KUBLAI KHAN, the grandson of GENGHIS KHAN. The invading Mongols brought with them a scale and a system of notation different from that used by the Chinese. This scale was as follows:—

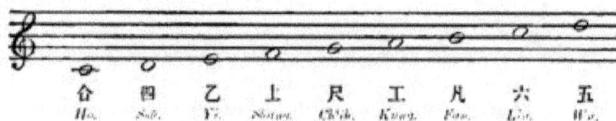

合	四	乙	上	尺	工	凡	六	五
Ho.	*Sah.*	*Yi.*	*Shang.*	*Ch'ih.*	*Kung.*	*Fan.*	*Liu.*	*Wu.*

This new notation rapidly became popular on account of the simplicity of the characters compared with the complicated signs of the ancient scale. But confusion was naturally created by some musicians using F natural, while others used F♯. KUBLAI KHAN, who always paid strict regard to the ancient laws and customs of the conquered Chinese, endeavoured to reconcile the two scales by introducing F♯ in the modern gamut under the name of 勾 (*kou*); and the following gamut became dominant during the rule of the Yüan (元) dynasty[1]:—

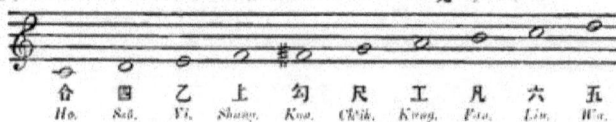

合	四	乙	上	勾	尺	工	凡	六	五
Ho.	*Sah.*	*Yi.*	*Shang.*	*Kou.*	*Ch'ih.*	*Kung.*	*Fan.*	*Liu.*	*Wu.*

[1] *See* 釋賀考 book 樂譜, chapter 英譜.

The Ming (明) (15th century) adopted the Yüan gamut, but excluded all the notes producing half tones, and so obtained a pentatonic scale composed as follows:—

合	四	上	尺	工	六	五
Ho.	*Szŭ.*	*Shang.*	*Ch'ih.*	*Kung.*	*Liu.*	*Wu.*

The present dynasty—the Ch'ing (清)—reverted to the Yüan gamut, leaving out, however, the note *Fan* (勾) which was the real *pien-chih* of the ancient scale. Their scale is given as follows:—

Actual Names of Notes.		Ancient Names of Notes.		Names of Lus.		Western equivalent Notes.	
Ho	合	*Kung* (1)	宮	*Hwang* (1)	黃		C.
Szŭ	四	*Shang* (1)	商	*Tai* (1)	太		D.
Yi	乙	*Chiau*	角	*Ku*	姑		E.
Shang	上	*Chih* (1)	微	*Chung*	仲		F.
Ch'ih	尺	*Chih* 2	微變	*Lin*	林		G.
Kung	工	*Yu*	羽	*Nan*	南		A.
Fan	凡	*Kung* (2)	宮變	*Ying*	應		B.
Liu	六	*Kung* 3	宮少	*Hwang* (2)	黃清		C.
Wu	五	*Shang* 2	商少	*Tai* (2)	太清		D.

From what precedes it may be seen that not only have the names of the notes been changed but also the principle of the scale is no longer the same. The two *pien* or half tones of the ancient scale are no longer in use; they have, it is true, never been well understood by the majority of Chinese, but now, to avoid all possible confusion, they have been carefully put aside. The present Chinese theoretically admit seven sounds in the scale, but practically they only use five, and that as well in ritual music as in popular tunes.

Only the modern names of notes are used.

The ancient denominations of the notes are now only met with in books. They are the scientific terms of the five sounds. The modern names are much easier, and besides present the advantage that by means of a little sign affixed to the left of the note, the octave higher is at once expressed: thus, Ⅰ is A grave, and ⅼⅠ becomes A acute.

Some instruments, as the *ch'in*, the *se*, and the *pien-chung* require, on account of their special construction, quite a different musical notation, which will be given further on.

Each of the primitive names of notes had a particular meaning. The Chinese, who are so fond of comparing and contrasting, could not fail to find some relation between the five notes and—

> The five planets : Mercury, Jupiter, Saturn, Venus, Mars.
>
> „ points : north, east, centre, west, south.
>
> colours : black, violet, yellow, white, red.
>
> „ elements : wood, water, earth, metal, fire.

The affinity of the five sounds with the five relations of men and things is explained as follows by the Chinese :—

1 . 宮 為 君 (*kung sha chün*). The note *kung* corresponds to the chief, the ruler the Emperor.

2 . 商 為 臣 (*shang sha chén*). The note *shang* corresponds to the minister.

3 . 角 為 民 (*chiao sha min*). The note *chiao* is related to the people, the nation.

4 . 微 為 事 (*chih sha shih*). The note *chih* represents the affairs of the State.

5°. 羽 為 物 (*yü sha wu*). The note *yü* represents material objects.

In our Western music the position of a note on the stave determines its pitch. In ancient Chinese music, with only five characters to represent the different sounds, it must have been next to impossible to read a written piece of music. By inspection of the scale given above, it may be seen that the modern Chinese have a special sign for nearly every note of their melodic system. Their characters not only express the sounds, but also indicate the pitch—that is, their position in the gamut. The music of the Chinese, like their language, is written in vertical rows of characters from right to left. They never trespass beyond the limits of 14 sounds; finding within the compass of that scale an infinite variety of tunes to which Chinese ears only can become accustomed.

Chinese musicians must often be puzzled when reading a new piece, there being no way of distinguishing a note from its octave. This defect has been remedied to a certain extent by affixing little signs indicating the octave higher; but this custom is not general, and, owing either to negligence or ignorance, many pieces are found in which there is no means of distinguishing the notes 上. 尺. 工 from their respective octaves. But, as will be seen, this is the least important imperfection of Chinese solmisation.

OF THE VALUE OF NOTES.

The Chinese have not for each sound several figures expressing its value or length. Their notes indicate simply a certain sound at a certain height, but leave the reader in the most complete doubt as to their value. Sometimes signs or dots are added on the right of a note to signify that it is to be held longer than the others, but still this system is not uniform, and is found only in manuscripts.

This is incontestably the weakest point in Chinese musical notation. The total absence of signs showing the value, the rests, the time, etc., makes it quite impossible to learn a tune by merely reading the written notes. The best Chinese musician could only conjecture the general form of a written piece shown to him for the first time; to be able to decipher it he must first *hear it played*.

The following are the principal arbitrary signs in use:—

1°. Some notes are written larger than the rest, to emphasise them.

2°. A space is left between two notes. This may mean a rest or the end of a verse.

3. Small dots are written after the notes, one dot for one time. For instance, 工 may be ♩. then 工. will be ♪. and 工 ... will represent ♫

OF THE RESTS.

A rest is denoted by little signs (✓ or ✗) placed in the same row as the notes, but its duration is merely a matter of taste, and must be learnt traditionally. A space left between two notes may indicate a pause.

OF TIME.

The only measure scientifically recognised by the Chinese theorists is that in four time. In practice, however, several measures are admitted, especially that in three time.

Each fourth time is indicated by a small circle (o) written at the right side of the note; the three other times are marked by dots (...). But time and measures are not always indicated, and this deficiency, together with the total absence of signs marking the value of notes, compels the musician to learn all the tunes by tradition. The tunes, modified by the individual taste of the performer, may after a lapse of time become quite different from what they were originally.

SONG CALLED 鮮花 (THE FRESH BEAUTIFUL FLOWER).

上. 尺. 工. 工. 工.
上. 尺. 六. 六. 工. 工.
尺. 六.. 工. 六. 六. 六.
工. 尺. 五. 五. 五.
士 五. 上.. 凡. 凡. 凡.
六.. 六. 六.. 凡. 凡.
尺 五. 五.
凡. 尺. 上. 五. 六.. 六..
五. 工. 六.
六. 尺. 五. 五.
工. 上. 工.. 工.. 六. 六.
尺. 合.
六... 士..

SIGNS OF ALTERATION OF NOTES.

The Chinese have nothing approaching what we call sharps, flats, or naturals—that is to say, signs which in a piece of music sharpen or flatten certain notes and produce those charming effects which constitute the beauty of our music. They remain faithful to their pentatonic scale, and find therein all the variations necessary to satisfy their ear.

In our music the number of flats or sharps at the beginning of a piece indicates the key-note or tone in which it is to be played. To attain the same end the Chinese state at the beginning of a piece to what lü—that is, to what tone—the key-note must correspond. This indication is used in sacred music only, this being the only scientific music of China. I give here an example of the Chinese signature.

The following piece is the part played by the flute—簫 (hsiao)—in the Spring Hymn to Confucius. According to a decree issued by CH'IEN LUNG (乾隆) in the eighth year of his reign, ceremonial services to CONFUCIUS were to be performed four times a year, and the same hymn sung every time, but in a different key:—

Foreign Equivalent.	Flute Part for the 春仲 (or Spring Ceremony).	Heading indicating the Pitch of the Key-note.	Explanation.
		夾 *chia*	} *kia-chung*, the 4th *lo* in the circular diagram = D ♯ or E ♭.
	佽 伍 佽	鐘 *chung*	} acting as
	佽 伍 佽	禹 *wû*	fundamental sound or tone
	佽 伍 佽	宮 *kung*	
	佽 仕 伍	倍 *pi*	a doubled *ying-chung* (the 12th *lo* of the primitive notes, being doubled becomes the 12th *lo* of the grave notes, or B ♮
	佽 佽	應 *ying*	
	佽 仕	鐘 *chung*	
	佽 伍	起 *ch'i*	} begins } begins } start- the the the intonation } tone } tunes.
	仕 佽	調 *tiau*	
	佽 佽	用 *yung*	"When" employing
	仕 佽	尺 *ch'ih*	the character 尺, that is, the musical note 尺 of G,
	佽 仕	字 *tzŭ*	}
	佽 伍	調 *tiau*	to intone a tone,
	佽 佽	除 *ch'u*	(we must exclude, leave aside,
	伍 仕	工 *kung*	the notes *kung* and *yi*, or
		乙 *yi*	A and E.

By means of the 12 *lôs* the Chinese are enabled to transpose their scale of 14 sounds in any of the 12 tones. For instance, our scale of C is for the Chinese the scale of *kia-chung*, and when we have music written in the tone of E ♭ the Chinese say it is in *chia-chung*. An important point to be observed is that, no matter in what tone a Chinese piece is written, the first sound or key-note is always 宮 (*kung*), the second *shang*, the third *chiao*, and so on. The best foreign equivalents for these five names would thus be:—

Tonic, or first degree, for *kung*; subtonic, or second degree, for *shang*;

Mediant, or third degree, for *chiao*; dominant, or fifth degree, for *chih*;

Subdominant, or sixth degree, for *gü*.

At the grand ceremonies Chinese musicians regulate their instruments according to one of the fixed instruments, as the *pien-chung*, the *pien-ch'ing*, or the *p'ai-hsiao*, three instruments which give exactly the same notes as the *lôs*. The heading or signature written before the music of the other instruments refers to them.

Thus, when the flute-player is warned by the heading of his music that *chia-chung* is to be considered as *tonic* or *kung*, he knows that the five-note gamut of those three instruments will be—

Chia-chung, chung-lü, lin-chung, ying-chung, pei ying-chung,
Kung, shang, chiao, chih, yü.

and he will play accordingly.

In their music the Chinese carefully avoid the *pien* or half tones. Therefore the notes creating half tones are named in the heading, that they may be excluded.

OF THE DIATONIC GAMUT.

In Western music we call the diatonic gamut a scale of seven degrees (eight with the octave), containing five full tones and two half tones. In the major scale the semitones are found between the third and fourth degrees and between the seventh and eighth. In the minor scale they are between the second and third and between the fifth and sixth degrees.

The Chinese gamut also contains eight degrees, but these being a series of perfect fifths brought within the compass of an octave, without having undergone any *temperament*, they form irregular intervals incompatible with our tempered instruments.

Experience teaches us, and it is proved mathematically, that if the following series of perfect fifths, C, G, D, A, E, is not tempered, the E last obtained will be found too *sharp* to form a *true* major third to the note C. Indeed, the third thus obtained is so sharp as to be absolutely offensive to the ear. If we continue the above series we shall find defects in all the other intervals.

To exemplify this assertion, let us suppose that the absolute length of a tube necessary to sound the note C or *huang-chung* is $\frac{1080}{729}$ parts of an inch, and let us take from the comparative table on p. 12 the notes necessary to form a diatonic scale; we shall have the following table:—

NAMES OF NOTES.				Required Length of Tubes to render the Chinese Notes,—stated in 120th parts of an Inch.	Required Length of Tubes to render the Foreign Notes,—stated in 120th parts of an Inch.	Comparison by Height of Lines.	
						Chinese.	Foreign.
Huang-chung	Liu	六	C	526.237	540		
Ying-chung....	Fan	凡	B	559.2	576		
Nan-lü	Kung	工	A	636	645.3		
Lin-chung	Ch'ih	尺	G	720	720		
Chung-lü..........	Shang	上	F	789.888	810		
Ku-hsi	Yi	乙	E	852	864		
Tai-tsu............	Szû	四	D	960	963.99		
Huang-chung	Ho	合	C	1080	1080		

The D, E, A, and B of the Chinese scale are too sharp, the F is nearly F ♯, and the octave C is unbearable to foreign ears. In practice, however, the Chinese are able to flatten or sharpen the notes according to requirements; but the intervals, the thirds principally, are never correct.

The third was long considered an imperfect consonance; it is only since the introduction of temperament that the third in Western music has been classified among the perfect consonances. The Chinese, like the ancient Greeks, recognise only the fifth, the fourth, and the octave as consonances.

If Chinese melody were accompanied by chords formed of their sharp thirds, the effect would be to a foreigner an intolerable cacophony. However, the melody of the Chinese being always unsupported, the dissonances are less apparent, and it approaches more closely to just intonation.

OF MAJOR AND MINOR.

Is the Chinese scale major or minor?

1°. In Western music the major mode is determined by the perfect major third on the key-note (e.g., C to E), and the leading-note (note sensible, B). Among the Chinese, the pentatonic, or five-notes' scale, is in general use, and this contains neither E nor B; there is consequently no major third and no leading-note.

2°. Our minor mode is indicated by a minor third on the key-note (say, A to C), and the leading-note (which should be G ♯). The Chinese scale offers nothing of the kind.

3°. Even if the heptatonic, or seven-notes' gamut, is used, the sharp third on C is more than a major third, and the third on A is an inexpressible interval.

Thus, being composed of irregular intervals, and having no leading-notes (without which there is no possible modality), the Chinese scale may be said to be neither major nor minor, but to participate of the two. Chinese melodies are not majestic, martial, sprightly, entrancing, as is our music in the major mode; and they lack the softness, the tenderness, the plaintive sadness of our minor airs.

The European writers on music who positively declare that Chinese music is major, have been misled by the rendering of Chinese tunes in Western notation. Indeed, Chinese music expressed in our notes and played on our instruments is not at all shocking; it may even be accompanied and sustained by chords and harmony. In this case there is no difficulty in declaring the music produced to be major or minor; but Chinese tunes so disguised no longer belong to genuine Chinese music, and cannot possibly afford conclusive proofs of anything concerning it.

OF THE CHROMATIC SCALE.

The Chinese have a scale composed of 12 semitones (that of the 12 *lüs*), which may be called the chromatic scale. This scale is used to transpose their diatonic gamut in any of the 12 keys, but never to play chromatic runs on the instruments, nor to write music proceeding with half tones.

Each degree is named from the *lü* producing its sound, but in its name only the first syllable is used. For instance, C (the first degree) is called *kuang*, for *kuang-chung*, and so on.

The 12 *lüs*, originally producers of those sounds, are nowadays unknown. Nevertheless, certain instruments created on the principle of the *lüs*, as the *pien-ch'ing*, the *pien-chung*, etc., are still in use, and are the guardians of the 12 semitones.

The transposition of the diatonic scale from one tone to another is very curious, and is worthy of the Chinese.

The scientific Chinese have a circular diagram (see page 9) on which the names of the *lüs* are written in order, with the names of the hours, moons, etc., to which they correspond. Supposing it is required to form a gamut of which *jui-pin* shall be the base; knowing the name of the tonic or key-note 蕤賓, which corresponds to the 5th moon), the Chinese musician will pass from it to the note six moons forward (thus, 黃 (*huang*), corresponding to the 11th moon); from this he will retrograde to the note four moons back (夷 (*i*), corresponding to the 7th moon); then he will go to the sound six moons forward (太 (*tai*) corresponding to the 1st moon); then four moons back again (無 (*wu*), 9th moon). He will thus create a scale of five sounds, 蕤 夷 無 黃 太, to which he will give the names *kung*, *shang*, *chiao*, etc.

If we put this pentatonic gamut in apposition to the corresponding Western notes, we shall have—

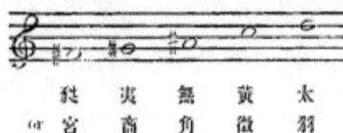

| 蕤 | 夷 | 無 | 黃 | 太 |
| or 宮 | 商 | 角 | 徵 | 羽 |

and it will be readily perceived that the C and D are nearly half a tone too flat; but to the Chinese this is no objection, their aim being to prove the irrefutable connexion of their music with astronomy and Nature.

Besides, when playing or singing the Chinese succeed perfectly in flattening or sharpening certain notes. The players on the *ch'in* are especially fond of producing such effects.

In ordinary popular music the existence of something resembling a chromatic scale is not even suspected.

OTHER SIGNS OF NOTATION.

Most of the instruments required in ritual music have a particular kind of musical notation adapted to the exigencies of their conformation. For instance, a piece written for the *ch'in* presents a complicated combination of strokes difficult to learn and to decipher. Still it is an ingenious and abbreviated kind of notation.

Neither time nor movement are ever mentioned at the beginning of a piece, and crescendos, decrescendos, legatos, etc., are utterly unknown to the Chinese.

OF SINGING.

It is difficult to give a correct idea of Chinese vocal music. Few foreigners are able to imitate Chinese vocalisation. The sounds seem to proceed from the nose: the tongue, the teeth, and the lips have very little to do, except for the enunciation of some labial words. Besides, men and women generally sing in the kind of voice known as *voix de tête*. Chinese singing is always in unison, and usually serves as an accompaniment to the guitar.

In ritual ceremonies the singing is of a tender and plaintive character, in a kind of minor key. It is also in unison, and therefore bears a striking resemblance to the first Christian *cantus planus*. It is generally accompanied by a kind of minuet dancing, in which the different attitudes and evolutions of the performers must express to the eye what the voices and instruments convey at the same time to the ear.

A remarkable peculiarity in the Buddhistic service is that although all the chanters utter the same words and follow the same rhythm, still each sings in the key most convenient to his own voice.

In theatres the singing is mostly a kind of "recitative" couched in pompous and metaphorical language.

OF HARMONY AND CHORDS.

The Chinese have nothing like our harmony, taken in the sense of chords, counterpoint, etc. The only collection of different but simultaneous sounds recognised by them is that produced by playing two strings (at a distance of a fourth, a fifth, or an octave) together on the *ch'in*, the *sé*, or the guitar.

SECOND GATE OF THE CONFUCIAN TEMPLE, WHERE THE STONE DRUMS ARE PLACED

RITUAL MUSIC.

Under the name of Ritual Music must be comprehended all music performed at Court or at the religious ceremonies of the 儒 敎 (ju-kiao), or "Sect of the learned," of which the Emperor is the chief. These ceremonies take place at fixed epochs; for instance, the winter solstice is the fixed date for the worship of Heaven the summer solstice for that of Earth. During the spring and autumn lucky days are chosen for the worship of CONFUCIUS and the spirits of departed sages; at other times services are performed at the temples of agriculture, of ancestors, of the sun, of the moon, etc. Most of these ceremonies take place during the early hours of the morning, and are always terminated at sunrise. The Emperor is supposed to attend himself, but if for certain reasons he is unable to do so, he deputes one of the Princes or a high dignitary to conduct the ceremonies in the name of the sovereign. Everything connected with them is minutely regulated: the number of musicians, of dancers, of instruments, vases, and utensils of all kinds, of movements, genuflexions, and even words is rigorously fixed. As all the ceremonies are pretty much alike, I will illustrate only those performed at the temple of the great sage CONFUCIUS

CONFUCIUS (in Chinese, K'ung-fu-tzŭ), the great sage of China, was a native of the state of Lu (B.C. 550), the present province of Shantung, where his tomb can be seen at a place called Ch'ü-fou. His life and writings have been made generally known by numerous translations into various foreign tongues,[1] and therefore I need not explain how and why he became an object of profound veneration for succeeding generations

CONFUCIUS is now worshipped all over China by those who belong to the lettered class. In every prefecture and sub-prefecture there is a temple devoted to him, where ceremonies are performed with great pomp twice a year. The Confucian temple at Peking is a spacious and magnificent building, covered with a double roof of yellow glazed tiles, which is sustained by massive wooden pillars. Access to the temple is gained by passing through three great gates and traversing as many wide courts, where weeds are growing luxuriantly. Before the temple there is a broad, elevated, marble terrace reached by a flight of steps, and guarded by handsome balustrades of elaborately carved marble. The temple has three great doors, which are wide open at the time of worshipping. Within, on the north side of the great hall and facing south stands the shrine with the tablet bearing the words: The Most Holy Ancient Sage CONFUCIUS.[2] In two other shrines, facing, one west and the other east, are to be seen the tablets of the four principal disciples of the sage, MENCIUS, Tsĕ-ssŭ-tzĕ, Tsĕng-tzĕ, and Yen-tzĕ.[3] In two other large buildings lying east and west of the temple are placed, in the order of merit, the tablets of ancient worthies.

Before CONFUCIUS' shrine in the temple there are several tables bearing offerings of meats of different kinds, grains of all sorts, fruits, wine, incense, silk, satin, etc.

[1] See Legge's "Classics," among others.
[2] 至聖先師孔子.
[3] 亞聖孟子.述聖子思子.宗聖曾子.復聖顏子.

The way from the first gate to the centre of the temple is left open for the passage of the Emperor or his deputy, with his suite of princes, dignitaries, and attendants. At the second gate the Emperor leaves his sedan and walks to the temple at a slow, stately pace; a band of 14 musicians and 11 ensign and umbrella bearers precedes him, while an appropriate piece of music called 導引 (*Tao-yin*), the Guiding March, is played.

I give here this march which is played by two *shêng*, two *ti-tzŭ*, two *hsiao*, two *yün-lo*, two *tun-kwan*, two *drums*, and two pairs of castanets.

尺　四　合、　工　合、　工　　四
　　　工　　　工　六、四、
　　　六、　尺．　　五　工
合、　五　上、四　六　合
工．　六　四　合　工　四
合　工、　合、工
四、　　　工．　六、　尺
合　尺、　五　上　四、
工．　上、　四　六、　四　合。

導
引
樂
譜

In foreign notation this may be rendered somewhat as follows :—

THE GUIDING MARCH.

(The little circles and dots at the side of the Chinese notes and above the Western notes indicate that the drummers and castanet players must sound their instruments.)

When the Emperor enters the temple the guiding music ceases, and the most profound silence reigns for a while. Everybody is at his place: the singers, harpers, *shêng* players, and small drums are ranged on the west and east sides within the temple; the bell and stone instruments, the flutes, and the larger drums are outside, on the marble terrace are 36 dancers divided into two groups, one west and one east, and the dancers standing at equal distance one from the other; in front of each group is a leader carrying a kind of banner with which he guides the movements of his group; in front of the chanters in the temple are two dragon-embroidered flags called *hui*.

When the Emperor has arrived before the shrine, the grand master of ceremonies gives the signal to commence by beating the little drum he holds in his hand. At this signal the flags (*hwi*) are raised, the *chu* (leader) beats his instrument three times, and the whole band begins to play.

The following hymn is the only one sung in honour of CONFUCIUS, according to a decree issued in the eighth year of CH'IEN LUNG (A.D. 1743). The same words and the same music are always used, the only difference being the change of *lü* or key-note. The hymn is always sung in the *lü* corresponding to the moon during which the ceremony takes place; for instance, during the second moon *chia-chung* is assumed as *lü*, and during the eighth moon the key-note is *nan-lü*. The hymn is divided into six stanzas :—

    1. 迎 神 *ying shn'a*, receiving the approaching Spirit.
    2. 初 獻 *ch'u hsien*, first presentation of offerings.
    3. 亞 獻 *ya hsien*, second presentation.
    4. 終 獻 *chung hsien*, third and last presentation.
    5. 徹 饌 *ch'e chuan*, removal of the viands.
    6. 送 神 *sung shn'a*, escorting the Spirit back.[1]

A remarkable peculiarity of Chinese worship is the firm belief that the spirits in whose honour a ceremony is performed descend from heaven to receive the offerings prepared for them. Therefore here the first stanza is devoted to inviting and meeting the Spirit :—

Very slow.

_[1] I continue to say the Emperor because if he does not officiate himself the ceremony is always carried on as if he were present.

_[2] For translation of this Hymn see p. 34.

4

During the second strophe the Emperor kneels twice and knocks his forehead three times on the ground; he then presents the fruits of the earth and the wine. The chanters sing :—

合其	工清	四春	乙俎	合展	日生	尺玉	工于	
四香	尺酒	四秋	合豆	四也	合民	合振	合懷	初
合姑	合既	尺上	工千	乙大	尺未	工金	四明	獻
工升	工載	四丁	乙古	四成	乙有	尺聲	乙德	

Very slow.

Yi hsei ming ti. Yu chin chin shing.

Shing ming wi ya. Chau yeh te ching.

Tsa tao ch'a ku. Chin chin shang fong.

Ch'ing chiu chi tai. Ch'i hsiang shih shing.

During the third strophe the Emperor kneels twice and knocks his forehead three times against the ground; he then offers the sacrificial animals, which have previously been stripped of their skins, cleansed, and placed on the tables. The singers chant —

乙相	尺禮	合犉	乙黼	乙誠	尺犇	尺升	工式	
四覬	乙陶	工髦	乙黼	尺孚	乙協	乙堂	合禮	亞
合而	合樂	尺斯	四雍	乙鼎	合發	合再	四莫	獻
工善	四淑	工彥	四雍	工獻	四豐	乙獻	乙愆	

Shih li mo ch' in. Shing l'ang tsai l'an.

During the fourth strophe the Emperor again kneels twice and knocks his forehead three times against the ground; then he presents incense, pieces of silk, satin, etc., which are burnt in the tripod incense-burner. The chanters sing:—

尺至	乙彝	合惟	乙惟	尺於	乙皮	尺先	工自	
乙今	乙倫	尺聖	尺天	乙論	乙弁	乙民	合古	終
合木	尺攸	合時	工鼐	四思	合祭	合有	四在	獻
工釋	工敘	四若	乙民	合樂	工菜	四作	乙昔	

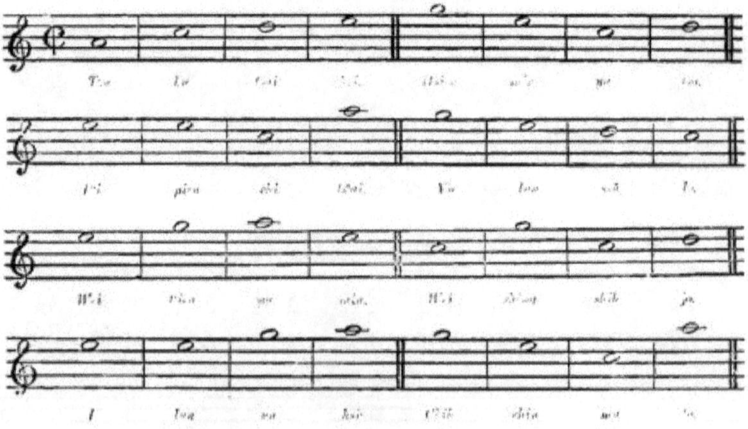

During the fifth strophe the flageolet remains standing before the tablets, while assistants remove the vessels from the hall. The singers say:—

乙中	乙樂	乙冊	乙禮	合嘻	合四	仜祭	工先	
四原	尺所	四疏	尺成	四敢	尺則	合師		徹
合有	合自	合冊	合不	合曼	仜受	四有		候
工薦	仜生	仜宸	乙徹	仜肅	尺宮	乙福	乙言	

During the sixth and last strophe the spirits are supposed to take their departure. The singers say:—

合育	仜化	仜祀	乙聿	合流	尺兢	尺沬	工曷	
四我	乙我	尺事	尺昭	四澤	乙行	仜泗	合繹	送
合膠	仜蒸	合孔	合祀	乙無	乙行	合洋	四峨	神
工庠	尺民	四明	仜事	四彊	尺止	四洋	乙峨	

Hoo   oo   ch'ng   wie.   Ya   oo   chiew   hsiaay.

During the second, third, and fourth strophes the dancers perform their evolutions. During the first and last two strophes they remain stationary in a respectful position. By the word *dancing* is not meant anything like the foolish jumping or endless turning to be met with in our ball-rooms; the dancers are grave performers who by their attitudes and evolutions convey to the eye the feelings of veneration and respect which are expressed by the words.

EVOLUTIONS MADE BY DANCERS DURING THE HYMN.

FIRST.

SECOND.

THIRD.

FOURTH.

FIFTH.   SIXTH.

SEVENTH.   EIGHTH.   NINTH.

TENTH.   ELEVENTH.

In ancient times also dancing held a conspicuous place in worship, having been first introduced into the ceremonies by the Emperor Shun (B.C. 2255). It was not till the third year of Yung-ming in the Ch'i dynasty (齊 永 明) (A.D. 483) that an imperial decree ordered that dancing should form part of the Confucian ceremonies.[1] There were at first only civil dancers (文 舞), but the Emperor Chēn Kuan (貞 觀) of the T'ang (唐) dynasty (A.D. 650) introduced also military dancers (武 舞). The civil dancers, dressed in their court uniform, had in one hand a long feather and in the other a small stick; the military officials who took part in the dance were dressed in full military uniform, and had in one hand an axe and in the other a shield. Under the present dynasty the military dancers have been excluded, and the number of civil dancers has been fixed at 36, with two chiefs. The long feather called 翟 (ti), which was anciently composed of three feathers bound together in the form of a trident, has also been reduced to a single peacock's feather. The little stick, called 籥 (yüeh), which the dancers hold in the left hand, was anciently a flute with three holes, on which they played at intervals; now it is a simple stick.

The hymn is sung by two groups of three singers standing east and west of the temple and facing each other. The pitch of the key-note is given them at each strophe by the bell instrument. They are accompanied by the other instruments in the following way:—

The tê-chung, or large bell, sounds the first note of each verse.

The pien-chung, or bell-chime, gives one sound at each word, and, in fact, guides the voices. After the bell-chime the lutes give their note, which is followed by all the other instruments except the pien-ch'ing, or stone-chime, which is struck after all the other instruments, in order " to receive the sound and transmit it " to the second note, which is treated in the same way.

At the end of a verse a drum is beaten three times and answered by another drum, after which the bell-chime gives the key-note and the next verse is begun.

When the hymn is finished the head of the yü, or " tiger-box," is beaten once, and a stick is passed rapidly along the projections of its back.

The Emperor then retires, preceded again by the band playing the "Guiding March," and at the second gate he enters his chair.

From what precedes it is easy to realise that a ceremony performed during the quiet hours of night, and with all the requirements of the rites, is really worth seeing; and the profane who can contrive to be admitted to a quiet corner cannot fail to be deeply and solemnly impressed.

[1] See 釋 奠 考, book 舞 譜.

TRANSLATION OF THE SACRIFICIAL HYMN TO CONFUCIUS.

1.—RECEIVING THE APPROACHING SPIRIT.

Great is Confucius!
He perceives things and knows them before the time;
He is in the same order with Heaven and Earth;
The teacher of ten thousand ages.
There were lucky portens, and on the unicorn's horn a tuft of silk.
The rhymes of the song correspond to the sounds of metal and silk.
The sun and moon were unveiled to us;
Heaven and Earth were made to look fresh and joyful.

2.—FIRST PRESENTATION OF OFFERINGS.

I think of thy bright virtue.
The jade music ends. The music of metal is first heard.
Of living men there never was one like him;
Truly his teaching is in all respects complete.
The vessels are here with the offerings, the same as during thousands of years.
At the spring and autumn equinoxes, on the first of the days whose character is 丁 (ting),
Clear wine is offered.
The sweet smell of the sacrifice now first rises.

3.—SECOND PRESENTATION.

The regular sacrifices should be offered without deficiency.
The chief sacrificer advances in the hall and presents the second offering
The harmonious sounds are heard of drum and bell;
With sincerity the wine cups are offered.
Reverently and harmoniously
Approach the sacrificers, men of honourable fame.
The ceremonies are purifying, the music cleanses the heart;
They work on each other and reach the point of perfect goodness.

4.—THIRD AND LAST PRESENTATION.

From antiquity through all the ages
Primitive men have done this.
They wore skin hats; they offered of the fruit of the ground.
How orderly was the music!
Only Heaven guides the people;
Only the Sage conforms his instructions to the day and hour.
The moral duties are arranged in their proper order.
Till now the wooden clapper sounds.

5.—REMOVAL OF THE VIANDS.

The ancestral teacher said in his instructions:
"Those who sacrifice obtain happiness."
Throughout the four seas, in students' halls,
Who would dare not to be reverential?
The ceremony concluded, the removal of the offerings is announced.
Let none be neglectful or show want of respect;
Let their joy be in him who is the source of their culture;
Let them remember the poem of the beans in the fields, and imitate him.[1]

6.—ESCORTING THE SPIRIT BACK.

The Fu and Yi mountains are very high;
The Chu and the Ssŭ spread their waters far,
So thy beautiful acts extend their influence above and around,
Causing benefits without end.
Now has been seen the glory of the sacrifice;
The sacrifice has been made to appear great and beautiful.
He renovates the thousands of our people;
He fosters our schools and halls for instruction.

[1] *Chung yüen ya sho.* This is found in the Book of Odes: "The beans grow in the fields. The people gather them. The *ming ling* has a family of crubs. The wasp carries one away on his back. In instructing your children, take care to imitate this good example."

POPULAR MUSIC.

Under this designation must be understood all theatrical, ballad, processional, and ordinary street-song music.

To perform this music none but common instruments are used: the moon-shaped guitar, three-stringed guitar, two-stringed violin, clarionet, drums, castanets, etc. In the principal cities there are concert-halls, to which Chinese are admitted for a few cash to hear a song or a ballad. The orchestra ordinarily consists of two balloon-shaped guitars (played by girls who sing at the same time), one three-stringed guitar, one or two violins, one small drum to beat time, one flute, and one *yang-k'in*. All these instruments play, or at least try to play, in unison; still it seems to a foreigner not acquainted with their music that each performer has a part of his own, and that each aims to distinguish himself above his colleagues by making as much noise as he can. The impression produced on foreign ears is anything but favourable. Still, if patient attention be paid, it is soon discovered that the performers play in time and well together.

A CANTONESE ORCHESTRA.

Professional musicians, like actors, generally belong to the poorest classes of society. In Peking they are for the most part blind men; in Canton nearly all the musician-girls are blind, except courtesans living in "flower boats." It need scarcely be said, therefore, that the majority of the Chinese professional musicians are totally ignorant of the principles and theory of music. The only notation they make use of is the one known as the 工 尺 *(kung-ch'ih)*, or "common notation." Music is little practised as a recreative amusement among the Chinese lower classes, but this may be attributed to the fact that they are always so busy, so hard-working, so gain-seeking, that they find no idle time to devote to pleasure; still it not unfrequently happens that when passing along the streets towards evening one hears the strains of a fiddle coming from one shop or another, and should curiosity then lead one to enter, he might find the shopkeeper or his assistant busily engaged in quite a different pastime from that of selling candles or sugar loaves. That music is much liked in China is proved by the numerous bands of musicians which parade the streets; by the least important festival being never celebrated without music of some kind; by the constant singing in the streets of children, domestics, hawkers, and passers-by. What does it matter that we foreigners find the popular music detestable if the Chinese themselves are contented with it? Is not contentment the first step towards health? And is not health the condition *sine quâ non* of happiness?

Well-organised theatrical performances only came into use during the Tang (唐) dynasty. The dances which had prevailed up to that time had become so licentious that the Emperor YÜAN TSUNG (元宗) (A.D. 720) thought it necessary to prohibit them; and in their place proper theatrical representations were instituted.

Theatrical pieces are divided into acts or 折 *(che')*, and are often preceded by a prologue or 揳子 *(sie-tze)*, in which the various personages come on the stage to explain their names, qualities, and the part they are to play.

Singing is the privilege of the principal actor in the piece. He represents generally a person of great virtue and moral qualities, and his singing consists in pompous eulogies of what is good and commendable. The singing is not unfrequently in the "recitative" style, and the way the orchestra accompanies, in broken, sudden chords or in long notes, bears a striking resemblance to our European recitative.

Mr. G. C. STENT, of the Chinese Maritime Customs, wrote some years ago a very well-thought and well-rendered article on "Chinese Lyrics."[1] The comparisons between Chinese and foreign songs are admirably drawn, and are full of wit and humour. I propose to introduce here some of Mr. STENT's paragraphs including some of the songs translated by him. I have, however, taken the liberty to replace the music which he has given by the *real* and *correct* tunes, which I have myself carefully noted down from hearing them played.

MR. STENT says:—

"We are all aware that the Chinese are, as it were, an isolated race, and will not allow the privacy of their homes to be ruthlessly invaded by their own fellow-countrymen and friends, much less by foreigners. How, then, can we obtain a knowledge of their everyday domestic life; how know anything of the thoughts, sentiments, feelings, affections, actions, and the thousand little nameless nothings that help to make a Chinese home? . . . . . As we are now situated, the knowledge of Chinese domestic or home life is only to be obtained from three sources—novels, theatricals, and songs. . . . In them foreigners can see Chinese as they really are; see the interior of their homes, have their daily life vividly depicted, even to the minutest detail; hear their endearing expressions. . . . . Much may be learnt from theatricals. I do not mean what I should call their spectacular pieces, made up of gorgeous dresses, ... and fighting, but modern farces or comedies; in them you see a good deal of Chinese life and manners, and pick up many a quaint expression or curious custom. A great play upon words is also often exhibited in them; absurd mistakes occurring through the similarity in the sounds of characters; so that for punning purposes I think the Chinese language is unequalled. . . . . . . The songs

[1] See "Journal of the North-China Branch of the Royal Asiatic Society for 1871-72," page 93.

I shall introduce . . . . . I have obtained, some for the sake of the music, which I have fancied pretty; others, for the (what I have thought) beauty of the language; others, again, for their absurdity. Here I may remark that foreigners in this case are very like Chinese. How many songs are published nowadays that are downright trash—utterly worthless but for the fact that some of them have pretty tunes. How many persons play the airs of or sing popular songs when they know the language of them is simply idiotic. Who cares to know that

> 'Captain Jinks of the Horse Marines
> Fed his horse on corn and beans,'

or that some individual, name unknown, 'feels like a morning star,' which he takes care to repeat an alarming number of times, the only drawback to his otherwise blissful state of existence being the pertinacious attacks of a fly, which he endeavours to dispose of summarily by using terms at once entreating, reproachful, and stern? I quote his own eloquent words, 'Shoo! fly, don't bother me.' Yet this kind of song is patronised extensively; but I trust in the majority of cases only for the music, which is really cheerful and pleasant, for it would be showing a poor taste for poetry to say one admired the language. So that however simple or absurd any song I introduce may appear, I claim that it possesses equal, if not superior, advantages to some of our own popular songs; for there is something not generally known to foreigners to be learnt from every Chinese song, and the music of some is positively pretty, and would compare favourably with some of our own ballad music. . . . . Songs or ballads in Chinese are very similarly arranged to our own, and the mere rhymist would find it an easy matter to string a number of rhymes together, on account of the construction of the language and the immense number of characters having similar sounds; whether they could write poetry or not is another matter. . . . . . I shall at once proceed . . . with the translation of a song called 'Wang ta-niang,' or, as we should say, 'Dame Wang.' I have perhaps been free in the translation, and have utterly repudiated the possibility of my being able to put it into English verse. . . . . .

WANG TA-NIANG OR MADAME WANG.

"The translation runs thus:—

FIRST VERSE.

呀 外 怠 紗 窗 紗　唱
隆 叮 响 兒 壁 隔　姐
呀 誰 誰 問 兒 隔
娘 大 王 兒 壁 隔
橙 高 了 在 門 進 娘 大 了
　　　 咳 合 一 合 一 程 白
地 賤 個 這 我 到 不 呀 易 上
　　　　　　　 了 上

From the outside of the gauze windows
Came the sound of a neighbour's tapping.
The girl within exclaimed, 'Who is it?'
'Tis your neighbour, WANG ta-niang!'
Dame WANG entered the door, and sat down on a high stool.
Heigh-ho! heigh-ho!

Girl (*log.*): 'You treat me lightly by not coming oftener to my poor place.'

SECOND VERSE.

啊 帳 蓉 芙 開 撇　唱
香 粉 脂 是 兒 開
呀 被 綾 紅 呢 瞧 瞧
娘 姑 二 的 瘦 娘 姑
樣 人 個 和 不 了 樣
　　　 咳 合 一 合 二
呢 了 樣 怎 天 幾 這 娘 姑 二　白

D.W.: Drew the flower-embroidered curtains,
Inhaled the fragrance of the cosmetics,
Turned down the red damask counterpane.
Looked at the girl,
And perceived that she had fallen away to a mere shadow.
Heigh ho! heigh-ho!

D.W. (*log.*): 'Well, Miss, and how have you been these last few days?'

THIRD VERSE.

哪 天 幾 這 奴 奴　唱
轆 輾 又 延 延 茶
剛 用 忘 撒 也 也
餐 愛 不 呀 也 假 茶
了 用 難 實 可 我　假 茶
　　　 咳 合 一 合 一
罷 瞧 瞧 來 生 召 個 請 你 與　白

Girl (*sings*): 'For the last few days I have had no energy or life whatever,
With no inclination even for my tea,
And no appetite whatever for my food,
For both tea and food I have felt such repugnance that I have had great difficulty in taking them.
Heigh-ho! heigh ho!'

D.W. (*log.*): 'Shall I call in a doctor to look at you?'

FOURTH VERSE.

呀 他 請 不 奴 奴　唱
他 要 不 也 家 奴
呀 來 生 召 個 請
捏 捏 又 捏 捏
了 怕 害 奴 是 可 捏 捏 呀 捏 捏
　　　 咳 合 一 合 一
罷 來 侍 和 個 請 你 與　白

Girl (*sings*): 'I'll not call in one, for I do not want him.
If I were to send for a doctor, he would only be feeling my pulse and sounding me;
And I am afraid of feeling and sounding.
Heigh-ho! heigh-ho!'

D.W. (*log.*): 'Shall I send for a Buddhist priest for you?'

FIFTH VERSE.

唱 奴家不請他呀
奴家也不要他
請個和尚又兵兵
可是奴害怕了
兵兵呀兵兵

GIRL (*sings*): 'I'll not send for *him* either, for I do not want him.
If I invite a Buddhist priest, he will only be jingling and banging;
And I am afraid of jingling and banging.
Heigh-ho! heigh-ho!'

白 與你請個喇嘛從來

D. W. (*loq.*): 'Shall I call in a Lama priest for you?'

SIXTH VERSE.

唱 奴家不請他呀
奴家也不要他
請個喇嘛又喧喧
可是奴害怕了
喧陵合一合一

GIRL (*sings*): 'I'll not call *him* either, for I do not want him.
If I send for a Lama, he will only be singing and chanting;
And I am afraid of singing and chanting.
Heigh-ho! heigh-ho!'

白 與你請個魔杖從來

D. W. (*loq.*): 'Shall I call in an exorcist for you?'

SEVENTH VERSE.

唱 奴家不請他呀
奴家不要他
請個魔杖又喃喃
可是奴害怕了
喃喃陵合一合一

GIRL (*sings*): 'I will not send for *her* either, nor do I want her.
For if I called in an exorcist, she would repeat spells and incantations;
And I am afraid of spells and incantations.
Heigh-ho! heigh-ho!'

白 這個不要那個也不要你這病是怎的呢

D. W. (*loq.*): 'You don't want this, and you don't want that; how did you get this sickness of yours?'

EIGHTH VERSE.

唱 三月裡呀
三月是清明
桃花開兒呀
楊柳發青又
王孫公子他可遊春景了
陵合一合一

GIRL (*sings*): 'The third month, ah! in the third month,
At the 'pure and bright' period,
When the peach blossoms were opening,
And the willows were bursting forth into green,
I met a young gentleman who was taking a spring stroll.
Heigh-ho! heigh-ho!'

白 遊春不遊春與你何干呢

D. W. (*loq.*): 'Spring stroll or not, what had that to do with you?'

NINTH VERSE.

唱 他又紅
又是俊家
奴家愛他呀
少年學生
我合句幾挑的情活了
陵合一合一

GIRL (*sings*): 'He loves me, for I am a fair and beautiful girl;
And I love *him*, too, for he is young and a student,
And I have spoken a few words of love to him.
Heigh-ho! heigh-ho!'

白 挑情不挑情你怕不怕媽媽知道

D. W. (*loq.*): 'Love or not love, are you not afraid of your parents knowing it?'

TENTH VERSE.

唱奴的爹爹呀
七十有單八
他耳聾眼又花
白不怕那二人
暖合一合一
座道知蟾哥你怕不

Girl (sings): 'My father is seventy-eight years of age,
And my mother is deaf, besides her eyes are dim:
I am not in the least afraid of them.
Heigh-ho! heigh-ho!'

D.W. (boy): 'Are you not afraid your elder brother and his wife will know it?'

ELEVENTH VERSE.

唱奴的哥哥呀
常常不在家
奴的嫂嫂啊
常常住娘家
暖合一合一
白不怕你姐妹知道麼

Girl (sings): 'My elder brother is seldom at home,
And his wife is constantly at her mother's house;
So I am not at all afraid of those two either.
Heigh-ho! heigh-ho!'

D.W. (boy): 'Are you not afraid of your sisters knowing it?'

TWELFTH VERSE.

唱奴和的姐姐呀
差不大
奴年少的妹妹啊
不知斜
那都是一樣的話
了
暖合一合一
白你與咱怎麼探呢

Girl (sings): 'Between my elder sister and myself there is no great difference,
And my younger sister is too young to know anything.
And you and I express the same opinions.
Heigh-ho! heigh-ho!'

D.W. (boy): 'And what is it you wish?'

THIRTEENTH VERSE.

唱穿著王大娘啊
你認乾老媽媽
姐妥下忙跪呀
那件乾老告媽媽
選了我與兒亦成全罷了
暖合一合一
白成全不了呢
唱成全不了那是可苦咱死了
暖合一合一

Girl (sings): 'Oh! my dear Mrs. Wang, I look upon you as my adopted mother' (hastily falls on her knees).
'On my knees I entreat you to be so in reality, and arrange this affair successfully for me.
Heigh-ho! heigh-ho!'

D.W. (boy): 'And if it cannot be completed successfully?'
Girl (sings): 'If it cannot be completed, then I shall die of bitterness.
Heigh-ho! heigh-ho!'

"I fancy," says Mr. Stent, "some of my hearers saying 'What rubbish!' Yes, it is rubbish. And yet there is a great deal to be learnt from this song, puerile as it appears in English,—more so than could be learnt from the two 'popular songs' I just now quoted; for in this we discover that there is amongst the Chinese, as with us, sickly sentimentality—love-sickness, in fact,—and we learn, moreover, the superstitious remedies suggested. First, the doctor (I do not include him of course under the head of 'superstitious remedies'); the young lady knows well that all the doctors in the world, with their pulse-feeling; priests, with their banging of cymbals, etc.; Lamas, with their chantings; and exorcists, with their incantations, are useless. She is afraid of all these characters, but, from various causes, she is not in the slightest degree afraid of her own family. Another thing we learn, that there is such a thing as 'sweethearting' or love-making amongst them; it may be indulged in by stealth—a great deal is done in that way in our own countries; but it remains a fact, in spite of father, mother, or friends, she meets this young gentleman, and actually tells him she loves him, and to all appearance, too, without his even asking her, though for the credit of the fair sex I trust he may have done so, although she omitted mentioning it. At another place she says, 'He loves me because I am beautiful; and *I love him*,' not because he is handsome, but because 'he is young and a student;' this shows that although young ladies may not study themselves, they like those who do. So here we have mutual love among this ceremonious people; 'He loves me and I love him;' and to wind up all, if the girl does not succeed in marrying this young gallant, we have the promise of her dying of bitterness—in other words, dying broken-hearted.   .   .   .

"The next song I shall introduce is called, as I shall translate it,—

THE HAUNTS OF PLEASURE, OR "YEN-HUA-LIU HSIANG."

Yen - hua - yu - - - lia - - - hsiang.

N - - - chea - - - dhai.

yû - - Liu - - dhü - - Kwan - - ja - Tsi - chi - hau - da

Pai - yü - Hao - nü - hsiang - - nu - - lai. Ha! ha! ha!

ha! ha! ha! ha! ha! - - - Ai - yü - i - ta - kai - gü - Ch'oi.

Ch'i - R. - lou - chao - - p'ai. - - Ha! ha! ha! ha! ha! ha! ha! ha!

There are in all 13 verses in this song, but I give here only the Chinese text of the first verse :—

蒼梢呀花烟

呀釵裙女

粉官擦臉

呀開兒花肌紫

來女仙似好

咳咳咳

呀咳呼一呀咳

牌招攬了起扯

咳咳咳

This song is also known under the name 十五朵花 *(Shih-wu to hwa)*. "The Fifteen Bunches of Flowers."

Mr. STENT continues :—

"One would not imagine by the tune that the words of this song related to a very painful subject. There is a pathos and plaintiveness in the language which are very affecting, and most of the ideas are conveyed figuratively. I will not attempt to translate it, for indeed I feel I could not do justice to it, so I will simply give a general outline of it. . . . . . . A girl bemoans her hard fate, and bitterly reproaches her parents for their hard-heartedness and covetousness in selling her, when quite a child, to a life of infamy. She, in pathetic language, describes her progress step by step in guilt, and the many incidents connected with such a life; flattered and caressed if successful, beaten severely with a whip if the reverse, till, as she touchingly expresses it, 'the tears trickled down my poor little face;' on to old age, with youth and beauty gone, everyone looking on her with contempt, no friends or relations to notice her, the son to burn incense for her when she is dead; what has she to hope for? Winding up with a prayer to heaven to protect her and send someone to take her from that horrible life, enable her to be virtuous, so that she may get on the road to heaven. There is something peculiarly pathetic in this song, and much also to reflect on, for we learn from it that girls are remorselessly sold by their parents to a life of infamy; probably two-thirds of the unfortunate beings we see being sold in a similar way, very few indeed taking to it by choice. What struck me most . . . . . was the earnest prayer at the end of the song. No talk of 'chin-chin-ing Joss,' but a direct prayer to heaven. There is something inexpressibly touching also in another part; she almost reproaches heaven for giving her the 'peach-blossom destiny' when she exclaims, 'Heaven's heart must have felt resentment against me, or why allow the two characters "peach blossom" to alight on me? Why not cause them to fall on some other person? Surely, in my former life I could not have cultivated virtue?' To understand this my hearers must bear in mind that in Chinese fortune-telling certain characters are lucky or unlucky, as the case may be; and the two characters 桃花, 'peach blossom,' are considered particularly unlucky, for if they fall on a male child it is believed he will grow up a prodigate, if a female, that she will become fallen; so that parents consider it ominous of the future fate of their children, should they be so unfortunate as to have a 'peach-blossom destiny.'

Mr. STENT gives several other songs and ballads, but not having been able to verify the music, I refrain from inserting them here.

6

The following air is exceedingly popular in North China; it is entitled 媽 媽 好 明 白 (*Ma-ma hŏ mi'ng-pei*), "Oh, mamma! you understand me well."

The following ballad is called 十 二 重 樓 and contains no less than 48 couplets. However, the first couplet only is given here:—

Moderato. ORCHESTRA.

VOICE.

正 月 是 舊 年
Chĕ̆ng yŏ-ĕh shĭh hsin   uĭ-en

ORCHESTRA.

正 月 是 新 年
Chĕ̆ng yŏ-ĕh shĭh   hsin-uĭ-en

VOICE.

丈 夫
Chăng fu

In conclusion, I give the two tunes played ordinarily at funeral and nuptial processions. Both are exceedingly original and really worthy of a better interpretation than that afforded by the shrieking clarionet.

Funeral March.

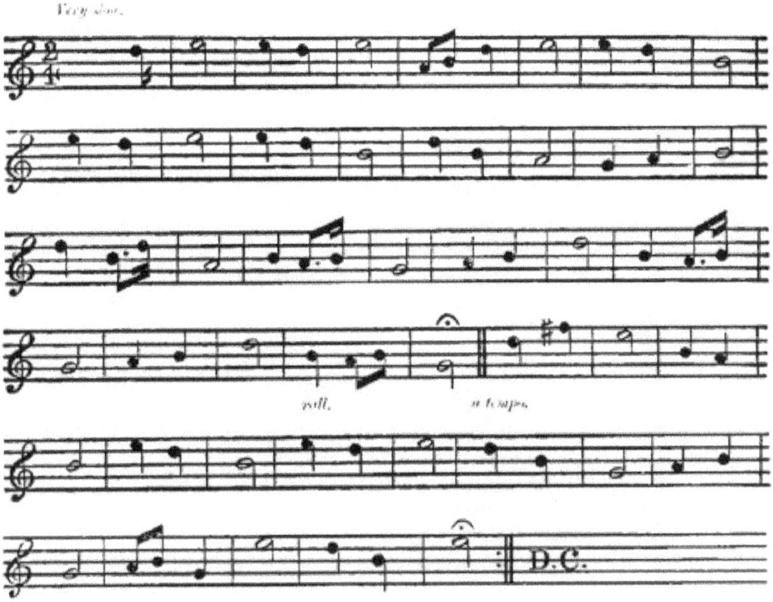

Wedding March.

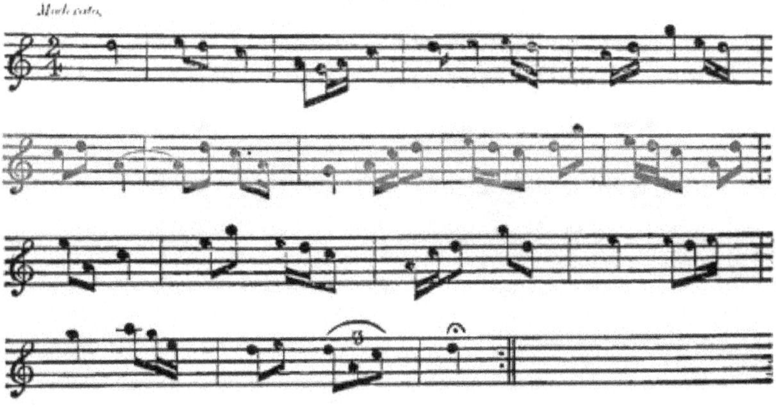

DESCRIPTION OF INSTRUMENTS.

Chinese musical instruments might be divided into two distinct categories—first, those of a somewhat complicated workmanship, used in the ritual ceremonies, and which are held sacred; and second, those of a common, primary form, used in popular music. But in order to keep in accord with the poetical spirit of the Chinese, I will follow the classification adopted by them.

It has been said above that according to Chinese ideas music is nothing but the expression of the perfect harmony existing between heaven, earth, and man. The numerous comparisons derived from this principle have also been mentioned. If the Chinese imagined the existence of certain resemblances or affinities between music and creation; if they found the idea of their system in natural phenomena; if they discovered in the 12 moons and the 5 planets the basis of their 12 *lūs* and 5 notes; finally, if the 神理 *(shǎ'n-li)*, or spiritual principle of music, was derived from heavenly regions, it is evident that the instruments (which represent the 氣 數 *(ch'i-shu)*, or material principle) were to be found in the natural productions of earth.

The Chinese therefore put Nature under contribution for the production of eight kinds of instruments corresponding to the eight symbols 八卦 *(pa-kwa)* of Fŭ Hsī, which, they believe, are the expression of all the changes and permutations which take place in the universe.

I give here a table showing the order of the sonorous bodies, with the symbols, the points of the compass, the seasons, and the instruments to which they correspond:—

No.	Sonorous Bodies.	Kwas or Fŭ Hsī's Symbols.	Points of the Compass.	Seasons.	Instruments.
1	Stone	乾 *Ch'ien*	N.W.	Autumn–winter	The stone-chime.
2	Metal	兌 *Tuī*	W.	Autumn	The bell-chime.
3	Silk	離 *Lí*	S.	Summer	The lute.
4	Bamboo	震 *Chên*	E.	Spring	The flute.
5	Wood	巽 *Hsün*	S.E.	Spring–summer	The tiger-box.
6	Skin	坎 *K'an*	N.	Winter	The drum.
7	Gourd	艮 *Kên*	N.E.	Winter–spring	The reed-organ.
8	Earth	坤 *K'un*	S.W.	Summer–autumn	The porcelain-cone.

In the following description the instruments will be grouped under one of the above eight categories, according to the material they are made of, but they will also be distinguished by a consecutive series of numbers, which will unite them in one whole group.

1. STONE.

The use of sonorous stone to make musical instruments may be said to be peculiar to China. At all events, the Chinese were the first to give stone a place in music; their classics frequently mention the stone-chime as being known by the ancient Emperors and held in great esteem. Unfortunately, of the music and the instruments in use during the Hsia, Shang, and Chou dynasties, nothing remains but a few books which escaped the destruction ordered by the Emperor SHE HUANG-TI;[1] and under the Emperor CHÊNG TI (成帝) (B.C. 32) a complete stone-chime was discovered in a pool, where it had been thrown, and from this model new chimes were made.

The best stone for chimes is said to be jade, but another kind of black calcareous stone is generally preferred, because it is easier to work and comparatively much cheaper.

No. 1.—The *T'ê-ch'ing* (特磬), or "single sonorous stone," is a stone cut in the shape of a carpenter's square, and supposed to render the sound of the triple octave below *huang-chung*. The side which is to be struck by the performer's hammer measures 2.25 feet; the other side is only 1.8 feet in length. It is suspended in a frame by means of a string passing through a hole bored at the apex. It is also known under the name of 離磬 (*li-ch'ing*), perhaps on

[1] 可知三代之樂厎壞於秦 etc. *See* 蒐洛志樂.

account of its sound being so deep. Its place at the Confucian ceremonies is outside the temple, on the left side of the "Moon Terrace." Its use is to give one single note at the end of each *verse*, in order to "receive the sound."[1] Formerly the stone was cut in a fantastical form, representing some monstrous animal, fish, dragon, or the like. According to the "Illustrated Description of the Instruments of the present Dynasty"[2] there are 12 *K'ich'ing*, one corresponding to each of the *lüs*; and they are employed only at the religious and court ceremonies.

No. 2.—The *Pien-ak'ing* (編磬), or "stone-chime," is an instrument composed of 16 stones suspended on a frame. The stones, which measure 1.8 feet one way and 1.35 feet the other, are all of equal length and breadth, and differ only in thickness; the thicker the stone the deeper the sound.

Formerly the size of the stones was in a gradually diminishing progression, following the degrees of the scale of the *lüs*. The number of stones has also not always been the same. The ancient Chinese used 16 stones; the Hans, 19; the Liang, 21; the Wei, 24; the Northern Chou, 14; the Ming, 24. K'ANG HSI reverted to the old custom, which, besides, had been the one prevalent during the Chin (晉), Sung (宋), Ch'i (齊), and Sui (隋) dynasties.[1]

The music for the *pien-ch'ing* is expressed by means of the names of the 12 *lüs*, but only the first syllable of each name is used, as *huang*, instead of *huang-chung*; *ta*, instead of *ta-lü*, etc.

In ancient times the 16 stones represented the sounds of the 12 ordinary *lüs* and of the first four *lüs* of the acute series. The present dynasty has abolished the four acute *lüs* (the four 清 (*ch'ing*) as they were called), and in their place the four *lüs* immediately below *huang-chung* have been selected; these are called 倍 (*pei*), that is, double. The scale of the *pien-ch'ing* is actually as follows:—

Upper Column.

The notes of the upper column correspond to the *yang lüs.*

Lower Column.

The notes of the lower column correspond to the *yin lüs.*

To illustrate further the notation of the *pien-ch'ing's* music, I give here the part which this instrument has to perform during the first strophe of the Hymn to CONFUCIUS:—

Huang-chung is to be the key-note and the Double *I-tsé* is to begin the air.

(The sign V means that the Chinese equivalent note is nearly ¼ tone higher than the sound represented by the Western note. The ∧ means that it is nearly ¼ tone lower.)

[1] See 釋奠考.

In this *pien-ch'ing* piece the Chinese note 倍夷 *(pu-i-i)* cannot be properly rendered in foreign notation, because it is in reality higher than A♭ and lower than A♮; the same occurs with the note 夷 *(i)*, which is lower than G♯ and higher than G♮.

It has been already said that in the transpositions of the tones to form the different scales the intervals do not remain the same; this is due to the Chinese scales being formed of perfect fifths brought into the compass of an octave.[1] But the reader may ask, why do the Chinese not use the note 倍南 *(pu-i-nan)* (A) instead of 倍夷 *(pu-i-i)* (A♭), and the note 林 *(lin)* (G) instead of 夷 *(i)* (G♯)? Because the two notes proposed correspond to the *yin lü* series, and when the key-note of a scale is a *yang lü*, all the notes composing that scale must absolutely be *yang lü*; and when the key-note is a *yin lü*, all the notes have to correspond to the *yin lü*. There is no other explanation, and the Chinese aim is attained, viz., to prove the irrefutable connexion of their music with astronomy and Nature.

The *pien-ch'ing* is exclusively used in court and religious ceremonies; it would be considered a profanation to use it elsewhere. There is one of these instruments in each Confucian temple and imperial place of worship in the Empire, and no doubt the imperial palaces and residences contain many of the best kind; but it is impossible to find a complete *pien-ch'ing* for sale, although separate stones may be found.

At the Confucian temple this instrument is placed on the west side of the temple, on a line with the *te-ch'ing*. Its special part is to give one sound at the end of each word, in order to "receive the sound" and transmit it to the next word.

It is not known to whom and to what dynasty the invention of the *pien-ch'ing* may be attributed, but there is no doubt that it is one of the most ancient instruments.

No. 3.—The *Ko-ch'ing* (歌磬), or "singers' stone-chime," which has now totally disappeared, was an instrument the same in principle as the *pien-ch'ing*, with these exceptions: it was composed of either 12 or 24 stones, which were cut in fantastical forms; the pitch was

---

[1] The Chinese recognise the necessity of flattening or sharpening certain notes to adapt them to a change of key. Compare the "Eclysis" and "Ecbole" of the Greeks.

7

an octave higher, and the notes, instead of following each other in two series of *yin* and *yang* sounds, were placed in a chromatic succession.

No. 4.—The *Yü-ti* (玉笛) and the *Yü-hsiao* (玉簫) are two flutes, exactly the same as the ordinary flute; the only difference being that the material employed is marble instead of bamboo. The Chinese think that stone is less susceptible to changes of temperature, and therefore is best adapted to preserve the real sound of the *lüs*. For description, see "4°. Bamboo," below.

No. 5.—The *Hai-lo* (海螺), or "conch," although not properly a stone instrument, is classified here for convenience. It is a large sea-shell of conical form, with a hole in the apex through which to blow. It is used only by soldiers, watchmen, etc., and principally for the same purposes as those for which we use the bugle in Europe.

2°. METAL.

Metal is one of the five elements. It comes from earth, say the Chinese, and still it is a substance of quite a different nature.[1] It was necessary, therefore, to give it a place in music, and this was done in the earliest ages, for we see in the "Miscellaneous Treatise of Prince Lü" (B.C. 300) that "the Emperor HWANG TI (B.C. 2697) ordered LING LUN to cast 12 bells to agree with the 12 *lüs* and the five sounds."[2] Bells are also frequently mentioned in the classics.

Bell-metal is composed of six parts of copper and one of tin. When melting, the alloy appears first to be of an impure dark colour, which, however, soon changes into a yellowish white; this colour gradually passes to a greenish white, and when this last colour has become green, the metal may be poured into the mould. The mould itself must be made exactly according to the proper dimensions, for "if the bell is wide and short, the sound will not reach a great distance; if the metal is too thick, it will emit no sound; if the mouth is too large, the sound will be too loud."[3]

Bells of all sizes, from those weighing more than 50 tons down to the small ones which swing on the eaves of pagodas, used to be found all over China. Some are ornamented with characters (mostly sentences in honour of Buddha), some with designs and symbols; some are round, some are square; and all are used mainly for religious purposes. At the door of each Buddhist temple a bell is to be seen, which the believers strike "to call the attention of the sleeping gods."

No. 6.—The *Yung-chung* (鏞鐘), or "large bell," ought to be 4.5 feet in height and have a mouth of 2.8125 feet diameter, gradually decreasing towards the apex. The Chinese say that it was made to correspond with a very big drum; the one was not to be used without the other, for the drum had to give the signal to begin and the bell had to announce the end of the hymn at the ceremonies. Though now no longer in use, both instruments are still to be seen. At the temple of CONFUCIUS, in the same court in which stands the hall are two small pagodas, one to the east, the other to the west of the hall and in front of it.

[1] 金生於土而別於土.
[2] 黃帝命伶倫鑄十二鐘和五音 etc. [8] 呂氏春秋
[8] 攝患恩志樂 vol. 8.

A CHINESE BELL TOWER.

In the east pagoda, to which access is gained by ascending a few steps, hangs a big drum, somewhat damaged by its exposure in the open air; and in the other pagoda on the west the large bell is suspended.

No. 7.—The *Po-chung* (鎛 鐘) is a single bell suspended upon a frame, and corresponding to the *tě-ch'ing*, or "single sonorous stone." When this bell sounds, the *tě-ch'ing* must answer.[1]

It measures 3.6 feet in length, and has a diameter of 2.25 feet, which gradually decreases towards the top. There are 12 *po-chung*, corresponding to the 12 *lüs*, and intended to meet the changes of key which occur according to the seasons. The measurements here given correspond to the *huang-chung*, or first bell. The *po-chung* is placed outside the temple (at the Confucian ceremonies), on the right side of the "Moon Terrace." It has to give one note at the beginning of each verse, in order to "manifest the sound"—in other words, to give the pitch. It is struck with a wooden hammer. It was called *sung-chung* during the middle ages.

¹金聲玉振金舂玉應

No. 8.—The *Pien-chung* (編 鐘), or "bell-chime," is an instrument composed of 16 bells suspended upon a frame. It is made on the same principle as the *pien-ch'ing*, or "stone-chime," and, like that instrument, is of the greatest antiquity. The Yellow Emperor— HUANG TI (B.C. 2697)—used a chime composed of 12 bells, agreeing with the *lüs*; the Chou

dynasty (B.C. 1100 to 255) had chimes of six and nine bells, decreasing gradually in size and diameter; of these, however, nothing remains but a meagre description in the native records.

In subsequent ages various kinds of chimes were made: some were composed of 24 bells, corresponding to two series of *lüs*; others of 16 bells, corresponding to the 12 *lüs* plus the first four *lüs* of the acute series; others of 14 bells, corresponding to the notes of the diatonic scale, C, D, E, etc.: in a word, this instrument underwent the same changes as the 'stone-chime."

Anciently the bells were quadrate: under the Tang (A.D. 600, and after) and subsequent dynasties the bells were oval and were adorned with mamme in groups of nine each; the mouth was crescent-shaped, and they were hung obliquely. The Sung (A.D. 1000) provided each bell with a knob, by which it could be hung in a vertical position. But K'ANG HSI, of the present dynasty, abolished the ancient forms and adopted round bells, ornamented with the *pa-kwa* symbols, and having on the top a dragon, by which they could be suspended. Chimes were made of 16 bells, all of the same size and diameter, but differing in thickness and weight. These are the chimes now in use.

The music, the pitch, the notation, etc., of the *pien-chung* is exactly the same as that of the "stone-chime;" and, like this latter instrument, it is exclusively devoted to court and religious ceremonies. Wherever a stone-chime is used, a bell-chime is requisite; they are necessary one to the other: the bell-chime sounds and the stone-chime answers.

At the Confucian temple the *pien-chung* is placed on the east side on a line with the *pu-chung*. It gives one note at the beginning of each word, to intimate the pitch to the singers.

No. 9.—The *Ko-chung* (歌鐘), or "singers' bell-chime," is now no longer in use. It was constructed exactly on the same principle as the *pien-chung*, but it sounded an octave higher. It was the companion of the *ko-ch'ing*. The bells were either 12 or 24 in number, and they were quadrate or crescent-shaped. The place of this instrument during the Confucian

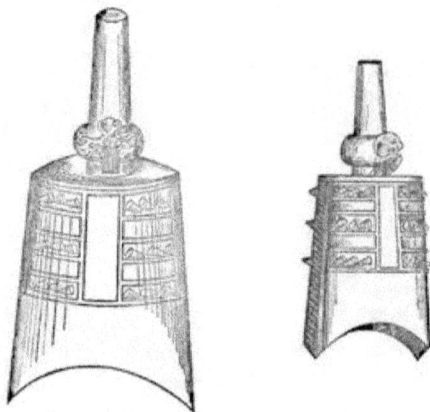

ceremonies was on the right side of the hall; it sounded one note at the beginning of each word. The *pien-chung* has now quite taken its place, and even single specimens of quadrate bells are seldom to be found.

No. 10.—The *Wei-shan* (維 謑) is a very ancient bell of the Chou dynasty. It had the shape of a balloon, and was suspended singly upon a frame. It was 1.35 feet in height; the

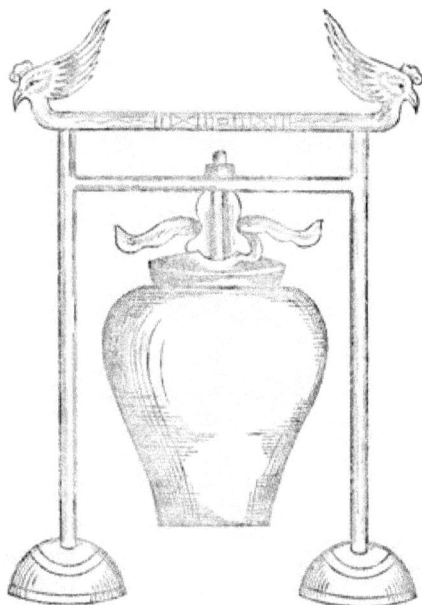

upper diameter was 1.1 feet, and the lower diameter measured 8.3 inches. It was suspended by a knob shaped somewhat like the 維 *(wei)*, monkey. This animal is said to have a yellowish grey head, a forked tail, and an upward nose; in rainy weather it hangs from the branches of trees by putting the two ends of its tail into its nostrils, and so forming a circle. From it was derived the Chinese idea of suspending their bells.

The *wei-shan* was used mostly for the ceremonies at the Temple of Ancestors, where it corresponded to some kind of drum which has also disappeared.

It has been said that this instrument "is simply a large bell, with small round bells suspended in it to act as a tongue, the sound thereby produced being exceedingly shrill."[1]

[1] N. B. DENNYS, "Journal of the North-China Branch of the Royal Asiatic Society, 1874."

No. 11.—The *Shou* (柷). This is the literary appellation of an instrument shaped like a mortar. The popular name is 椌 (*ch'iang*). It is struck with a wooden hammer, and when

used at the religious ceremonies is put into a kind of silk purse richly ornamented with costly fish scales. It ought to measure 1.3 feet in height and 9½ inches in diameter.

No. 12.—The *To* (鐸), or "tongued bell," is an ordinary bell having either a metal or a wooden tongue, and a handle at the apex. Formerly there were four different kinds of tongued bells in use in the army. The ringing of the *to* conveyed to the soldiers the injunction to stand still and be quiet in the ranks. Hence this bell came to be associated with the idea of respect and veneration; and when music was performed to illustrate the meritorious actions of warriors, faithful ministers, etc., the *to* was employed to symbolise obedience; each military dancer had a *to* with a metal tongue, and each civil dancer had one with a wooden tongue; it was used at the end of the dance.

At present the *to* is used only by bonzes to mark the rhythm of their prayers.

No. 13.—The *Lo* (鑼), or "gong," is cast in the shape of a platter or a Chinese straw hat with large brim; it is of various sizes, varying from 2 inches to 2 feet in diameter. It is suspended by a string, and struck with a mallet. The use of this noisy instrument is very general. At the gates of yamens it announces the arrival of visitors; in the army it gives the signal of retreat; in processions it frightens and drives away evil spirits; on board ship it announces departure; during eclipses "it frightens the heavenly dog when about to devour the moon"; in songs it marks the time; in the streets a small gong is the sign of the candy merchant, and a large one may announce the approach of the district magistrate with his retinue; in Buddhist temples it is beaten to call the attention of the "sleeping gods."

Native descriptions rarely mention the gong, perhaps because it is popular merely and is not required for imperial worship.

No. 14.—The *Yün-lo* (雲鑼), or "gong chimes," is an instrument composed of 10 little gongs suspended upon a frame by fine silk cord. The gongs are all of the same diameter, but they differ in thickness. The *yün-lo* is used at court, mainly on joyful occasions; at the

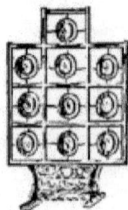

Confucian worship it is required only in the "Guiding March." It is to be seen sometimes at wedding and funeral processions, but it appears there simply for form's sake; the hired coolie who has charge of it for the occasion strikes pitilessly right and left, without regard for the tune his companions are playing. The specimen he carries is also very often a worthless one. It has become exceedingly difficult to find a *yün-lo* capable of giving a satisfactory gamut; besides, the pitch is not uniform, so that two *yün-los* rarely agree. The scale is ordinarily C, D, E, F, G, A, B, C, D, E, or, in Chinese notes, 合. 四. 乙. 上. 尺. 工. 凡. 六. 五. 化. The relative positions of the notes in the frame may be represented by numbers as follows :—

$$10$$
$$9 \quad 8 \quad 7$$
$$4 \quad 5 \quad 6$$
$$3 \quad 2 \quad 1$$

No. 15.—The *Po* (鈸), or "cymbals," are made on exactly the same principle as our Western instrument. They are said to have come originally from India.[1] The use of them

is most conspicuous (and particularly disagreeable to foreigners) at theatrical performances. After a quotation, a command, a verse, etc., the cymbals give 10 or 15 notes in rapid succession, and as the actor generally speaks in a falsetto, imitative voice, the words are almost inaudible.

No. 16.—The *Fäng-ling* (風鈴), or "wind bells," are small bells hung at the eaves of houses and pagodas, the clappers of which, having streamers attached, are swung by the wind. During the time of the Tang (唐) dynasty the *fäng-ling* was suspended in the examination halls.[2]

No. 17.—The *Hao-t'ung* (號筒) is a long cylindrical instrument having a sliding tube, which can be drawn out when wanted for use. In arrangement and form it is not unlike a telescope, but of much larger diameter. There are two distinct varieties. The first comprises instruments of different sizes made of wood and covered on the outside with copper; they are

exclusively used at funeral processions, and emit only one long grave note, which is heard at a long distance. The second variety includes instruments made of copper only; they are of a less diameter than the first and are used for military purposes.

[1] Compare with the Hebrew Metzilloth.
[2] N. B. Dennys, "Journal of the North-China Branch of the Royal Asiatic Society, 1874."

No. 18.—The *Lo-pa* (喇叭) is a long trumpet with a sliding tube similar to that of the *haut-boy*.[1] It gives four notes, C, G, C̄, Ē, and is properly a military instrument; but it is also the privilege of itinerant knife-grinders to use it to make known their whereabouts in the streets.

Another variety of the *lo-pa* is crooked, and therefore is called 札角 (*cha-chiao*); it is of various sizes and is used at wedding processions.

3 . SILK.

Silk holds perhaps the first place amongst the natural productions employed in music, not only on account of the great variety of instruments whose strings are made chiefly of silk, but also because stringed instruments can boast of the greatest antiquity. The classics and other ancient books make frequent mention of the *ch'in* and the *sê* in connexion with the first rulers of China; the descriptions which they contain are of the most exalted kind, and are full of allegorical comparisons, of which I will give an idea below.

No. 19.—The *Ch'in* (琴), is one of the most ancient instruments, and certainly the most poetical of all. It was invented by Fu Hsi, who called it *ch'in*, referring to restriction, prohibition,[2] because its influence checks the evil passions, rectifies the heart, and guides the actions of the body. The dimensions, the number of strings, the form, and whatever is connected with this instrument had their principles in Nature. Thus, the *ch'in* measured 3.66 feet or $\frac{366}{100}$ of an inch, because the year contains a maximum of 366 days; the number of strings was five, to agree with the five elements; the upper part was made round, to represent the firmament; the bottom was flat, to represent the ground; and the 13 studs stood for the 12 moons and the intercalary moon.

The strings also were subjected to certain laws. The thickest string was composed of 240 threads, and represented the Sovereign; the second and fourth strings contained each 206 threads; and the third and fifth 172 threads.

It is doubtful if all these remarkable similarities and comparisons are still adhered to and regarded. The *ch'in* of the present day retains the primary form, but the number of strings has been increased to seven. These strings pass over a bridge near the wide end, and then through the board, and are tightened by nuts below; at the smaller end they are tightened on two pegs.

The 13 studs should be of metal, the board of 桐 (*t'ung*) wood, and the nuts of marble or jadestone; and the silk should come from some particular place.[3]

[1] Compare with the Chatzozerah of the Hebrews and the Tuba of the Romans.
[2] 琴禁也禁止於邪, etc. See 爾雅.
[3] 削以峄陽之桐, 成以濮桑之絲, 徽以麗水之金, 軫以崑山之玉.

8

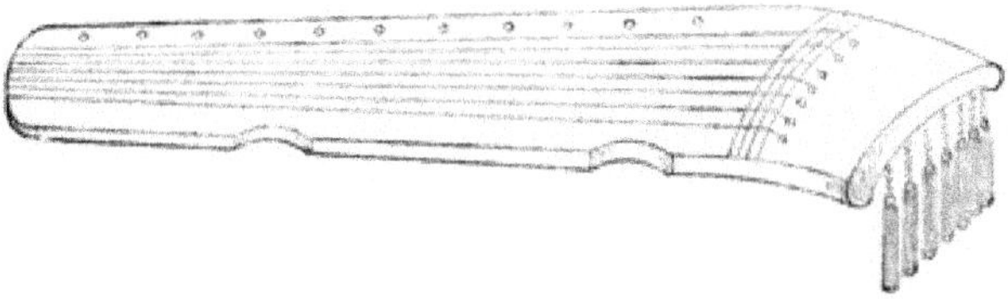

The *ch'in* is used for what is called elegant music (雅樂). It is supposed to be the special instrument of the educated classes; and yet, it is somewhat neglected by the present generation, being scarcely met with except at imperial ceremonies. This may be attributed to the fact that playing on the *ch'in* is surrounded with difficulties enough to deter the most willing learners. The notation, for instance, is quite peculiar: each note being a compound of several simple characters, so arranged as to convey at once to the eye of the performer the note to be played, the string to be chosen, the finger to be used, etc. The principal signs are the following:—

Right Hand.

卄 indicates that the right hand alone is to play the note.
一, 二, 三, 四, etc., indicate what string is to be played, the 1st, 2nd, etc.
毛 indicates that the thumb must push the string outward.
尸 " " " " inward.
乚 " " index outward.
木 " " " inward.
勹 " " middle finger " "
歹 " " " " outward.
丁 " " ring-finger inward.
乎 " " " " outward.
攵 two strings must be played at the same time, fifths or octaves.
厂 index must beat several strings in succession.
夯 same string must be played by the index and middle finger in succession.
尖 same string must be played by two or three fingers together, in order to re-enforce the sound.

Left Hand.

大 indicates the thumb.
人 " " fore-finger.
中 " " middle finger.
夕 " " ring-finger.
一, 二, 三, 四, etc., up to 十三, (*i.e.* Nos. 1 to 13) indicate at what stud the finger must press on the string.

These simple characters and a number of others are brought together in various ways to form compound characters. Thus, if the player meets with the character 葚,[1] he will know at once that he has to pull rapidly the seventh string forward and backward with the fore-finger; if he should meet the character 甃,[2] he would place the middle finger of the left hand opposite the seventh stud on the second string, and give an inward motion to that string with the middle finger of the right hand.

It is easily perceived that such complicated directions are difficult to learn and to remember, and that endless studies are necessary to master this instrument.

At the Confucian ceremonies there are six ch'in; three on the east side of the hall, and the three others on the west. The music which they have to perform is written in the simplest manner, but it is permitted them to embellish their part with all the difficulties which their skill will allow of.

Formerly the seven strings were tuned as follows:—

1	2	3	4	5	6	7
C	D	E	G	A	C	D

[1] Composed of 木 (index of right hand to be moved inward), ㄴ (index to be moved outward), and 七 (seven, i.e., the seventh string).

[2] Composed of 中, 七 (seven, i.e., the seventh stud), ㄱ, and 二 (two, i.e., the second string).

At present they are tuned as follows :—

1	2	3	4	5	6	7
G	A	C	D	E	G	A

The scale in the special notation is thus represented :—

筠 G, the 1st string to be pulled inward with the middle finger of right hand.
芶 A, „ 2nd   „
芶 C, „ 3rd   „
蒟 D, „ 4th   „
蒻 E, „ 5th   „
篋 G, „ 6th   „   outward with the fore-finger
篋 A, „ 7th   „

The following is the part of the *ch'in* in the first strophe of the Hymn to CONFUCIUS :—

Hwang-chung (C) is the key-note; *pei chē* (A) begins the tune.

No. 20.—The *Sê* (瑟) is said to have been invented by PAO HSI (庖犧), and to have had originally 50 strings. It is recorded that "when a certain Miss Sü (素) was one day performing on the *sê* in the presence of the Emperor HUANG TI (黃帝), the strains of the instrument impressed him so deeply and rendered him so sorrowful that he forthwith ordered the number of strings to be reduced by one-half."[1]

The *sê* is made on the principle of the *ch'in*, and, like that instrument, has been made the subject of numerous allegorical comparisons. The number of strings has varied, having been sometimes 27 or 25, sometimes 19 or 23 ; but the *sê* now in use has 25 strings. Each string is elevated on a movable bridge. These bridges represent the five colours; the first five are blue, the next red, the five in the middle are yellow, and then come five white, and lastly five black.

There are four kinds of *sê*, differing only in dimensions,—the longest measuring 84 inches.

          [1] *See* 爾雅 chap. 5.

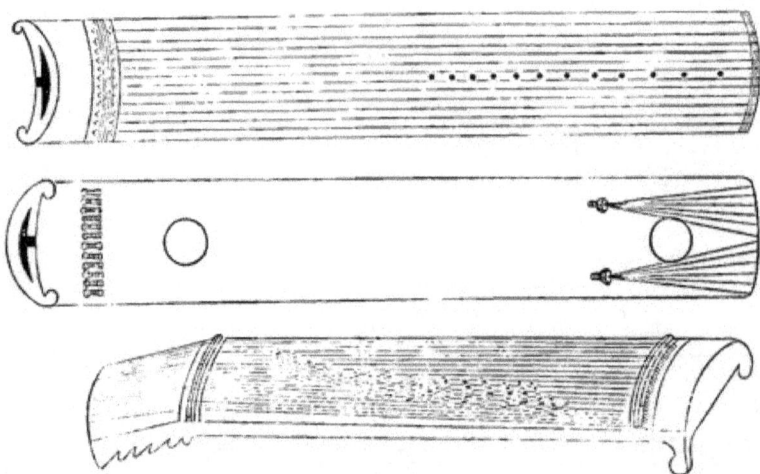

The sê is used chiefly at imperial and religious ceremonies. At the Temple of Confucius four sê are required; two on the east and two on the west of the hall. The notation is in principle the same as that of the *k'in*, but the characters are doubled, because the sê always plays two notes at one time. The scale of the sê is as follows:—

Each of these characters indicates which strings are to be played together. The *sè* when well tuned is supposed to give five octaves. Below is the part played by the *sè* in the Confucian Hymn, first verse:—

Hwang-chung (C) is the key-note; *pi-tsu* (A) begins the air.

No. 21—The *Tsang* (箏) is exactly the same as the *sè* in form and principle, but it is smaller and has only 13 strings, all elevated on movable bridges. It is used in preference to the *sè* at imperial receptions and on joyful occasions. The notation is identical with that of the *sè*.

No. 22. The *P'i-pa* (琵琶), or "balloon guitar," is about 3 feet long, and 1 foot wide in the body. It has four silk strings which are said to represent the four seasons. This and some other allegories enforce the belief that the *p'i-pa* has a more or less ancient origin but the date of its introduction is not known with certainty.

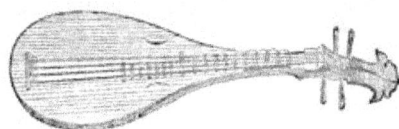

There is a slight difference between the instruments made in the South and those manufactured in Peking; the former are of better workmanship, but the fingering and the music are everywhere the same. On the neck table there are 11 or 12 frets, intended to guide the player. The strings are tuned C, F, G, C, or as the Chinese say, *ho* 合 *shang* 上 *ch'ih* 尺 *liu* 六.

This instrument being chiefly used on joyful occasions in connexion with the flute, the strings are of course tuned after the pitch of the flute; but in private the performer tunes it to the pitch which pleases him best.

In the South, the *p'i-pa* is the instrument preferred by troubadours who are hired to sing ballads, songs, etc.; and in the North it is generally played by men. The performer has to exercise great dexterity of finger and lightness of hand, for not only is the music always of animated movement, but nearly all the notes are played in *tremolo*, which effect is obtained by passing the nail or the plectrum rapidly forward and backward on the string.

By pressing the first string successively over all the frets the following scale is produced :—

Open string. 1st fret. 2nd. 3rd. 4th. 5th (the others are not used).

The second string produces :—

Open string. 1st fret. 2nd. 3rd. 4th. 5th. 6th. 7th. 8th. 9th. 10th. 11th.

The third string produces :—

Open string. 1st fret. 2nd. 3rd. 4th. 5th. 6th. 7th. 8th. 9th. 10th. 11th.

The fourth string produces :—

Open string. 1st fret. 2nd. 3rd. 4th. 5th. 6th. 7th. 8th. 9th. 10th. 11th.

The whole extent of the *pi-pa's* scale is therefore the following:—

But the frets which produce chromatic notes or half tones are never used. Probably in past ages, when music was cultivated as an art, these frets were employed to transpose airs into other keys; but it is nowhere recorded that they ever served to produce chromatic runs.

The *pi-pa* has no special notation. Being a popular instrument, and never required at religious ceremonies, it is played mostly by blind persons who acquire their musical knowledge by rote. There are, however, song-books for the *pi-pa* in which the ordinary notation (合, 四, 乙, etc.) is used.

No. 23.—The *Shuang-ch'in* (雙琴) is an octagonal guitar with a long neck furnished with frets. It is made of hard wood, and has four strings tuned in pairs, with the distance of a fifth between the two pairs. It is played with a plectrum; but it is now rarely used, the cost placing it beyond the reach of ordinary musicians.

No. 24.—The *San-hsien* (三弦), " or three-stringed guitar," has a shallow cylindrical body, the top and bottom of which are covered with snake skin. It has a long neck (without frets)

and three strings, which are tuned sometimes C, F, C (合, 上, 六), but more frequently C, D, A (合, 四, 工). It is sometimes played with the finger, but oftener with a plectrum. It is one of the favourite instruments of street ballad-singers.

No. 25.—The *Yüeh-ch'in* (月琴), or "moon guitar," is so called because the shape of the

body resembles a full moon; there is a variety, however, the body of which is octagonal. The neck, which is short, is furnished with frets for the convenience of the player. The four strings are tuned in pairs at the distance of a fifth. In some places the strings are made of copper instead of silk. This instrument is used, together with the *pi-pa* or *san-hsien*, to accompany ballads, songs, etc.

No. 26.—The *Hu-ch'in* (胡 琴), or "violin," has a hollow cylindrical body the upper end of which is covered with snake skin, while the lower is left open. The body is pierced by a long

arm, to which are attached four silk strings. These strings are tuned, the first and third 合 (or C), the second and fourth 尺 (or G). The bow passes between the strings, so that it requires close attention to play without touching the wrong string. The body is sometimes a round tube of bamboo, of wood, or of copper; sometimes it is octagonal in shape and is ornamented with little pieces of ivory. It is of varying size, the smallest having only two strings.

The *hu-ch'in* is rarely seen in the South, but in Peking it is one of the most popular instruments It is not difficult to learn (except the management of the bow), and it does not extend over one octave; moreover, it is comparatively cheap.

No. 27.—The *Êrh-hsien* (二 絃), or "two-stringed violin," is in principle exactly the same as the *hu-ch'in*, but it never has more than two strings. It is still more popular than the

hu-ch'in, for it is met with all over China. Its form varies. Sometimes it is a hollow bamboo tube, and is then called 呼 琴 (*ba-ha*); sometimes it is simply half a cocoanut shell, and is then called 椰 琴 (*yi-ch'in*); but no matter what its form may be or what material it is made of, it has always *only* two strings, which are tuned at a distance of a fifth from each other, and between which the bow passes.

The lower classes in China seem to be very fond of this rather unattractive instrument, of which foreigners have formed a decidedly poor opinion; but if we reflect that it is often played without taste or feeling, if we consider its cheapness and the simplicity of its form, and if we learn for ourselves that it is really capable of producing agreeable sounds, there will then be no reason to find fault with the inventor or the invention.

No. 28.—The *Yang-ch'in* (洋 琴), or "foreign harpsichord," has the form of a rectangular, trapezoidal, or oval box, about 2 feet long, 1 foot broad, and 4 inches high. When the lid which covers and protects the sounding-board is removed, one finds a range of fine metallic wires, disposed in sets of two, three, or four to each note, decreasing in length from the bass

upward, and fastened at both sides by nails. On the sounding-board there are two bridges
perforated with seven or eight holes each, over and under which the strings are stretched; and
the strings which pass over the first bridge have to pass through the opposite holes of the

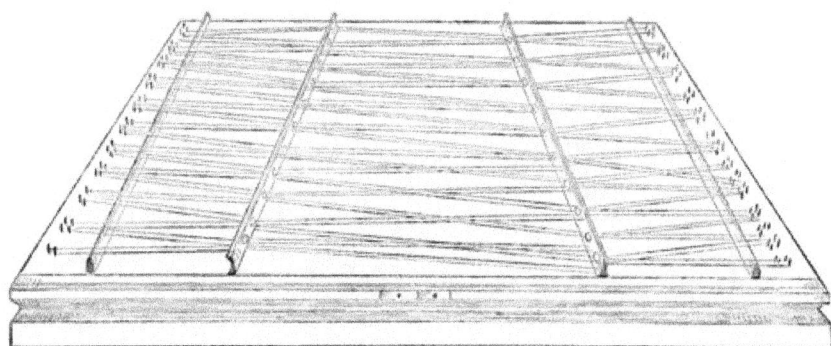

second bridge, and *vice versâ*. There are ordinarily 16 sets of strings, eight passing over the
right bridge and through the holes of the left bridge, and eight passing over the left bridge
and through the holes of the right bridge. This arrangement consequently affords four series
of notes, one on each side of each bridge; but only three series are in general use. The series
of notes given by the strings on the right side of the right bridge is not used.

The strings are tuned with a key in the same manner as our pianos. The scale produced
is the following:—

Left side of right bridge:

Right side of left bridge:

Left side of left bridge:

The *gaing-ch'in* is played with two light slips of bamboo, and it is capable of producing extremely pleasing sounds when well played. It may sometimes be heard together with the violin and the guitar, accompanying songs and ballads.

4°. BAMBOO.

One would think that bamboo ought not to be distinguished from wood; but, according to Chinese ideas, there is a very great difference between these two substances. Bamboo is neither properly a tree nor yet a simple plant, but it partakes the qualities of both these products. Its manifold uses have caused it to be considered a peculiar material, particularly useful in music.

No. 29.—The *Pai-hsiao* (排簫). The Chinese were a long time in discovering that a tube pierced at different places may be made to produce as many sounds as there are holes by merely stopping these holes one after the other. In order to get the various sounds, the ancient Chinese used as many tubes as there were sounds; these tubes fastened together produced the *pai-hsiao*, or "Pandean pipes." The first instrument of this kind was made by the Emperor Shun;[1] it was a collection of 10 tubes, gradually decreasing in length and connected together in a rough manner by silk cord. In subsequent ages the number of tubes was increased to 12, then to 16, and even to 24; at present, the *pai-hsiao* has invariably 16 tubes. These tubes are arranged upon a frame more or less carved and ornamented; they correspond to the 12 *lüs* and the first four *lüs* of the grave series, and emit exactly the same notes as the bell and stone chimes. The sounds of this instrument represent the

voice of the *fvng-hoang*, or phoenix; and the form of the frame typifies this bird with its wings spread.[2] The tubes which give the notes corresponding to the *yang lüs*, or

[1] 舜作十管詔簫. *See* 楊忠愍志樂.
[2] *See* 釋貧考.

"positive tones" are grouped together on the left side of the instrument; the *yin lüs*, or "negative tones," are arranged on the right side. The notes produced by the tubes, according to their position, are the following:—

1.   2.   3.   4.   5.   6.   7.   8.   9.

10.   11.   12.   13.   14.   15.   16.

The *pien-hsiao* is used only in ritual music. Two are employed at the Confucian ceremonies, placed respectively on the east and west sides of the hall. The music performed by them is exactly the same as that of the stone chime.

No. 30.—The *Yüeh* (籥) was a short flute with three holes, and blown at the end. Formerly it was used by the dancers, and was occasionally played to indicate their movements; at present, although the dancers still use the *yüeh* in their evolutions, it is no longer a flute but simply a stick.

No. 31.—The *Ch'ih* (篪) is a flute measuring about 14 inches in length. It is now blown transversely, but was formerly blown in the middle. The number of holes varies between 6 and 10, and even more. It has gradually become obsolete, its place being taken by simpler instruments.

No. 32.—The *Hsiao* (簫) is said to have been invented by a certain 耶 仲 (YEH CHUNG) during the Han dynasty.

This flute is a tube of dark brown bamboo, measuring about 1.8 feet in length. It has five holes above, one below, and one at the end, through which it is played. Flutes of this kind were formerly made of copper, of jadestone, or of marble, such materials being thought less liable than wood to be affected by changes of temperature. They were introduced into ritual music during the Yüan dynasty (*circa* A.D. 1300); and under the present dynasty their use has been confined to ritual music. At the Confucian ceremonies there are six *hsiao*, placed immediately outside the hall on the "Moon Terrace." The music which they perform is exactly the same as that of the other instruments, but it is noted in a different manner. The following is the ordinary scale of the *hsiao*:—

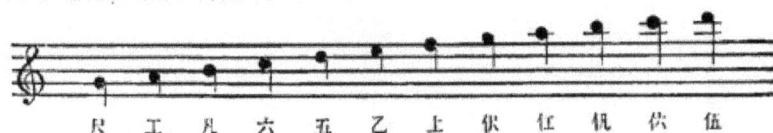

尺　工　凡　六　五　乙　上　伏　任　帆　伩　伍

(尺 — foreign D).

These notes are produced by stopping the holes one after the other, just as with European flutes.

No. 33.—The *Ti-tzŭ* (笛 子) is the flute ordinarily met with in China. It is a tube bound round with waxed silk and sometimes ornamented with tassels. It has eight holes: one to blow through, one covered with a thin reedy membrane, and six to be played upon by the fingers. There are, besides, several other holes at the end, but these are of no practical use except to attach the silk tassels and other ornaments. The fingering of this instrument is of course the same as that of all instruments of the flute kind, and the notation is the same as that of the *hsiao*, except that the *ti-tzŭ* is a fourth higher. This is the scale:—

六 五 乙 上 尺 工 凡 仸 伍 亿 仕 仸

(六 = foreign A, 902 vibrations per second).

The sounds emitted by Chinese flutes cannot properly be rendered in European notation, some being sharper and others flatter than the sounds represented by our notes; but this may be due as much to the ignorance of instrument-makers as to the irregularity of the intervals of the Chinese scale. Besides, the Chinese are not very particular in regard to pitch, and any shocking deficiency in justness of tone they manage to remedy by blowing harder or softer.

The *ti-tzŭ* is indispensable to every Chinese orchestra; it is used in theatrical performances, in funeral and marriage processions, and on various other occasions, both joyous and mournful. It is also one of the favourite instruments of courtesans.

Formerly all kinds of flutes blown transversely were called 笛 (*ti*). There were the *ch'iung-ti* (羌 笛), the shepherd's flute; the 橫 笛 (*hêng-ti*), the transverse flute; the 丑 笛 (*ch'ang-ti*), and the 短 笛 (*tuan-ti*), the long and the short flute. Some had four holes, some five, and some seven. Nowadays the form and number of holes of the *ti-tzŭ* are in all cases much the same. The only difference between the popular instruments and the flutes used in ritual music is that the latter are embellished with a dragon's head and a dragon's tail, an

addition not permitted in the case of ordinary instruments. Flutes thus adorned are called 龍 笛 (*lung-ti*), dragon flutes. Of these, six are used at the Confucian ceremonies; they are placed, together with the *hsiao*, three on each side.

No. 34.—The *Kuan-tzŭ* (管 子) is a small tube about 8 inches long. It has seven holes above and two below. It is blown by means of a coarsely made reed inserted at the upper end. Its sound cannot be said to be pleasing, at least to foreign ears. It is used mostly in funeral or marriage processions. It produces the following scale:—

The intervals of this scale suffer from the same defects as those of the *ti-tzŭ*. The 勾 (*kou*) is an ancient note no longer used. The 尺 (or G) of this scale corresponds as nearly as possible to the European A (902 vibrations per second).

No. 35.—The *Sona* (鎖 吶)—known to foreigners as the "Chinese clarionet"—is the most shrieking, the most detestable instrument used in China; and yet none is in more general use. When heard in the morning its sounds unmistakably announce a funeral cortège; in the afternoon, a nuptial procession.

The *so-no* consists of a wooden pipe fitted with a copper bell. It has seven holes on the upper side and one on the lower for the thumb. The mouthpiece is a small reed (like that of the European oboe) affixed to the upper end. It gives the following scale:—

上　尺　工　凡　六　五　亿　仕　伬

There are two varieties, differing only in size: the smaller kind is called 鎖箭 (*k'o-ti*). The 工 (*kung*) (or A) of the *so-no* is nearly identical with our A, 902 vibrations per second. The tunes played on this instrument at processions are in themselves very pretty and original, but the instrument is so false, and the ignorant player blows with so little regard to justness and softness, that it requires indeed great attention to detect and note them.

5. WOOD.

It is not known to whom the introduction of wooden instruments in music may be attributed, but wood is one of the productions of Nature so useful to man that it must have been given a place in music from the earliest ages.

No. 36.—The *Chu* (柷) resembles a square box, but it is larger at the top than at the bottom. It should measure at the top 2.4 feet on each side, and at the bottom 1.8 feet.

The height should be also 1.8 feet. But these dimensions are not adhered to. In the middle of the box there is a hammer, so contrived as to move right and left; and in one of the sides is a hole through which to pass the hand. The ancient *chu* was made of 梧桐 (*wu-t'ung*) wood. The interior is painted yellow, and the sides blue, red, black, and white. It is adorned with landscapes, figures of fabulous animals, etc. It is used only at religious ceremonies. At the Confucian temple there is one only, placed on the east side of the hall. It gives two sounds at the beginning of each strophe.

No. 37.—The *Yü* 敔, has the form of a tiger resting on a rectangular box. It should be 3.6 feet in length, 1.8 feet in width, and 1 foot high. The tiger has on its back 27

teeth, resembling a saw. At the end of each strophe the attendant strikes the tiger three times on the head, and rapidly passes his stick three times along the projections on the back, to announce the end of the strophe. The *yü* is placed on the west side of the Confucian hall.

No. 38.—The *Pai-pan* (拍 板), or "castanets," are two small slabs of a kind of red-wood 檀 木) attached together with silk cord, and on which a third slab of the same kind of wood is struck to beat time. These are in common use in popular orchestras. An ancient kind of castanet consisted of 12 small slabs of bamboo fastened together, upon which poetry was engraved; it was named 春牘 (*ch'un-tu*), and was used at religious ceremonies. Nowadays the *ch'un-tu* has been replaced at the Confucian ceremonies by another kind of castanet called 手 版 (*shou-pan*). The slabs of the *shou-pan* are of 槐 (*huai*) wood, 1.35 feet long, ⅛ inch thick, 2.5 inches broad at the lower end, and only 2 inches at the upper end. The words of the hymn are engraved on it. Each of the six singers has charge of one *shou-pan*; at each word they strike the slabs against the palm of the hand.

No. 39.—The *Mu-yü* (木 魚) or "wooden fish," is made of a block of wood hollowed out and shaped somewhat like a skull. It is painted red all over, and is of all sizes, up to 1 foot in

diameter. It is used by priests to mark time in the recitation of prayers when begging from door to door or in performing their ceremonies.

6. SKIN.

From the remotest ages the Chinese seem to have been acquainted with instruments of percussion, of which the tanned skin of animals was the vibrating medium. Drums made of baked clay, filled with bran and covered with skin, were the first in use. The idea of drums seems, however, to have come from the nations of Central Asia.[1] Of all the Chinese drums none are braced by cords : the skin is fastened on with nails.

No. 40.—The *Chin-ko* (晉鼓) is also called 大成鼓 (*Ta-ch'ing-ku*), because it is ordinarily placed on the left side of the *Ta-ch'ing* gate. At the Peking Confucian temple it is suspended in the eastern pagoda, and corresponds to the large bell hung in the western pagoda. It is about 5 feet in diameter.

No. 41.—The *Ying-ku* (楹鼓) is a drum suspended in a frame by four rings and beaten on the upper surface with two sticks. It is about 3 feet high and 2 feet in diameter. It is

richly painted and ornamented with birds, dragons, flowers, etc. Its place at the Confucian worship is on the east side of the "Moon Terrace." It is beaten three times at the end of each verse. Under the Sui (隋) dynasty this kind of drum was called 建鼓 (*chien-ku*).

[1] *See* 羯鼓錄 by 南卓.

No. 42.—The *Tsu-ku* (足鼓, also called 應鼓 (*ying-ku*) is a large drum, used at the Confucian ceremonies to correspond with the *ying-ku*. It is placed on the west side of the

"Moon Terrace," and is struck six times at the end of each verse, giving two beats in answer to each of the three beats of the *ying-ku*.

The *tsu-ku* is not quite so large as the *ying-ku*, and it is supported horizontally by a pedestal which raises it about 4 feet from the ground. For a long time this drum was out of use; but it reappeared again in the 13th year of CH'IEN LUNG (A.D. 1748).

No. 43.—The *Po-fu* (搏拊) is a small drum 1.4 feet in length, and 7 inches in diameter. The table on which it rests is 1 foot high. The *po-fu* is used only in religious ceremonies. At the Confucian temple there are two—one on the left, the other on the right side of the hall. In playing, the performer holds the drum on his knees and beats it with the hands. The *po-fu* gives three notes at the end of each verse answering to the two notes of the *tsu-ku*. The following are the three beats with the notation :—

     🔵 Beat the drum with the right hand.

     🔵   ,,   ,, left   ,,

     🔵   both hands.

搏
附

No. 44.—The *Taouka* (桃鼓) has a handle passing through the barrel. Two balls are suspended by strings from the barrel, and when the drum is twirled they strike against the

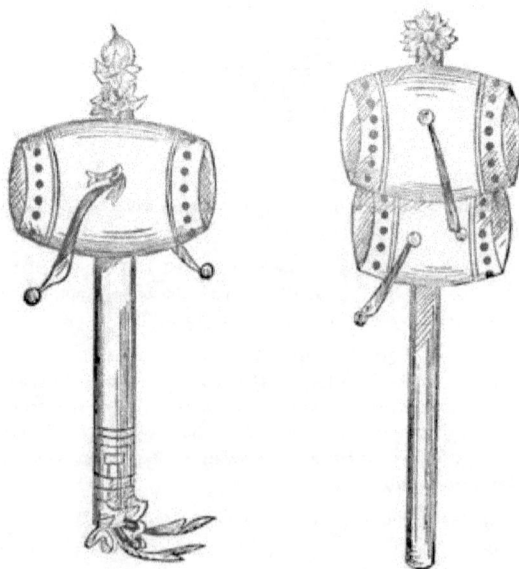

heads. Of drums of this kind used at the Confucian ceremonies there are two, placed on the east and west sides respectively; they are sounded three times at the end of each verse. They measure 1 foot in length and 1 foot in diameter. Anciently, the *tao-ku* used in ritual music was composed of two or more drums transfixed by a handle; sometimes it was composed of several

small drums hung together upon a frame, and struck only on one head by the balls. Such drums are now out of use.

The *tao-ku* is the special instrument by means of which the itinerant vendor of millinery goods makes known his whereabouts; but his drum is smaller and has generally a small gong on the upper side.

No. 45.—The *Pêng-ku* (梆 鼓) is a small flat drum, with a body of wood; the top is covered with skin and the bottom is hollow. The diameter of the head is about 6 inches. It rests on a wooden tripod. It is chiefly used in popular orchestras to beat time and accompany songs and ballads.

Besides the drums here enumerated, the Chinese possess several other kinds, varying from 5 inches to several feet in diameter. They have the "tambour de basque," the tambourine, and barrel drums of all kinds; some are richly ornamented with silk piece goods, some very simple and unadorned; but it would take too much space to describe them all.

7. GOURD.

The gourd was introduced among the musical instruments by the ancient Chinese to represent plants and herbs. It is called 匏 (p'ao), and its shell is at once thin and hard. Its hollow form rendered it available, and they made the *shêng*. Nowadays, however, wood has been substituted for the calabash, a change which does not seem to have made much difference in the sound.

No. 46.—The *Shêng* (笙) is an instrument intended to symbolise the *fêng-huang* or Phœnix. The body or wind-chest is made of gourd, or simply of wood, and in its upper part tubes of different length are inserted. These tubes are of five different lengths, and are so arranged as to resemble the tail of a bird, the middle tubes being the longest. The length of the tubes does not, however, make the sounds graver, for several of them have an aperture at a distance from the top which renders their length ineffective. The tubes in the lower portion are furnished with reeds exactly like those of our accordions; a little above the reeds the tubes are pierced so as to prevent their sounding, except by stopping the holes.

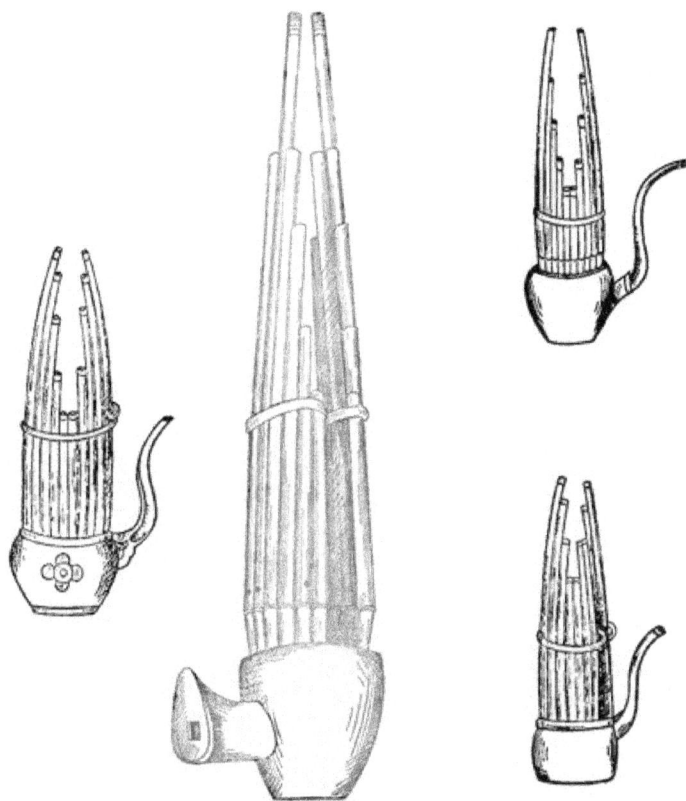

Dr. F. WARRINGTON EASTLAKE, whose designs of the different forms of the *shêng* I have here inserted, has made a special study of this instrument and has written extensively on the subject.[1] It is difficult to give a better and more complete description than his, and I will

[1] "China Review, August 1882.

therefore content myself with quoting the principal paragraphs of his work, only adding a few remarks where necessary:—

"The invention of the *shêng* is shrouded with the obscurity of the mythical ages. Tradition attributes its invention to a mythical female sovereign who succeeded Fú-hi, known as 女媧 (Nü-wo). Be this as it may, there can be no doubt that the *shêng* itself is of great antiquity; for not only do we find frequent mention of the instrument in the 'She' and 'Shoo-king,' but the commentators on ancient musical instruments invariably mention the great age of the *shêng*, and seem to delight in speaking of it as a proof of the inventive genius and musical talent of the ancient Chinese . . . . It may well be possible that the 排 簫 (*pai-hsiao*) (which *see*) was the prototype of the *shêng*. The date of the invention of the *pai-hsiao* must at all events be earlier than that of the *shêng*, to which it bears unmistakable resemblance . . .

"From the Classics we learn that the *shêng* held a leading position among the instruments which were in favour at the Imperial Court :—

> ' When to the Prince our way we've made,
> We sit and hear the organs played.'"

"The *shêng* is frequently mentioned in the 'Shi-king,' *e.g.*

> 'The lutes are struck, the organ blows
> Till all its tongues in movement heave.'[2]

> 'The drums loud sound, the organ swells
> Their flutes the dancers wave.'[3]

"According to the 'Erh-ya'[4] and 'Shuo-wên,'[5] there are, or rather were, two distinct forms of the *shêng*: the largest, and probably more ancient, known as the 巢 (*ch'ao*), or 'bird's nest,' the smaller known as the 和 (*ho*), or 'concord' . . . . . The scale of these two instruments must have been different, as the one had 19, the other 13 reeds . . . . . . The modern *shêng* differs in many essential points from the *ch'ao* and *ho* . . . . . . The *shêng* consists of three separate parts,—the gourd, the mouth-piece, and the . . . tubes. In shape the gourd is very much like a tea-cup, and about as large . . . . It is (sometimes) perforated at the base and inlaid with a small piece of bone or ivory, also perforated . . . . The 'gourd' was formerly made from a sort of calabash, but nowadays it is made of wood and lacquered.

"The mouth-piece consists of two separate parts,—the mouth-piece proper, made of wood, lacquered and inserted into the gourd, and a bone or ivory plate which covers the free end.

"There are 17 pipes in all. Every pipe, except the non-sounding or mute, 1, 9, 16, 17,[6] is composed of two pieces; the upper part bamboo, the lower part of some hard wood, probably teak. . . . . . . The lower part of each sounding-pipe is so cut as to admit of a small brass tongue, exactly after the model of European reed-tongues. The tongues . . are rudely fastened in with wax. Every sound-producing pipe has a slit on the inner side which serves to modify or intensify its tone. The tone of most of the reeds is rather sweet and soft, but some are harsh, and one or two almost inaudible.

"Each sound-giving pipe has a ventage which must be stopped by the finger in order to produce the proper note. This ventage is on the outside of pipes 2, 5, 6, 7, 8, 10, 11, 12, 13, 14, 15 ; on the inside of pipes 3 and 4 . . . . . . The pipes represent in all 11 notes. Pipes 2 and 6 produce the same note ; 12 gives the octave of 15, as does 13 of 14, and 11 of 7."

[1] "Shi-king', I., XI, 1.　　[2] II, I, 1.　　[3] II, VII, VI.　　[4] An ancient dictionary of terms.
[5] An ancient dictionary, published A.D. 100.
[6] Counting from the farthest pipe on the right side of the mouth-piece, 1, 2, 3, 4, etc.

The scale I have myself ascertained to be as follows :—

Notes:	尺	工	凡	六	五	一	上	伬	伍	仈	伬
Tubes:	15	7	5	14	4	3	2	12	11	10	13
					or		or				
					8		6				

The 尺 of the *shêng* is about our A (902 vibrations per second).

At the Confucian ceremonies there are six *shêng*, three on the east and three on the west side of the hall. They play exactly the same music and the same notes as the *ti-tzŭ*, or " flute." The *shêng* is never used in popular orchestras ; at nuptial and funeral processions the *shêng* is sometimes seen, but it is there merely for form's sake, in accordance with the requirements of the rites, and the hired coolie who carries it simply simulates playing.

Dr. EASTLAKE further says :—

"One very rarely hears the *shêng* nowadays, on account of a curious superstition. The Chinese say that a skilful performer on the *shêng* becomes so wedded to its music that he is ever playing ; but the instrument is played by sucking in the breath, and a long continuance of this brings on inflammation of the bronchial tubes and diseases of the lungs. So no performer is ever known to live longer than 40 years! The instrument, in playing, is inclined slightly towards the right shoulder : the forefinger of the right hand commands pipes 3 and 4, the thumb 2, 5, 6, 7. The other pipes are controlled by the first and second fingers and thumb of the left hand.

"That the *shêng* is one of the most important of Chinese musical instruments is apparent. No other instrument is nearly so perfect, either for sweetness of tone or delicacy of construction. The principles embodied in it are substantially the same as those of our grand organs. Indeed, according to various writers, the introduction of the *shêng* into Europe led to the invention of the accordion and the harmonium. KRATZENSTEIN, an organ builder of St. Petersburg, having become the possessor of a *shêng*, conceived the idea of applying the principle to organ stops.

8'. EARTH.

It was of absolute necessity that earth, the common mother of all things, should occupy a respectable place in music, and therefore the *hsüen* was invented.

No. 47.—The *Hsüen* (塤), or " Chinese ocarina," was invented by PAO HSI (庖羲) some 2,700 years before our era.

It is a reddish-yellow cone of baked clay or porcelain, ornamented with designs of dragons, clouds, etc., and pierced with six holes: one at the apex to blow through, three in front, and two behind.

When played, it is held firmly with both hands. According to a native description, it emits the following sounds:—

工　六　五　乙　上　尺

and at the Confucian ceremonies the two *hsüen*, placed one on the west and the other on the east side of the hall, play the same music as the *hsiao* flute. But as it is almost impossible to procure a specimen of this instrument, we have to rely on Chinese accounts of it.

CONCLUSION.

The question is often asked—Why does not Chinese music leave a better impression on the ears and minds of foreigners? Most naturally because it has not been made for foreigners. But from a theoretical point of view we may say that it is because:—

1°. The intervals of the Chinese scale not being *tempered*, some of the notes sound to foreign ears utterly false and discordant.

2°. The instruments not being constructed with the rigorous precision which characterises our European instruments, there is no exact justness of intonation, and the Chinese must content themselves with an *à peu près*.

3°. The melodies being always in unison, always in the same key, always equally loud and unchangeable in movement, they cannot fail to appear wearisome and monotonous in comparison with our complicated melodies.

4°. Chinese melodies are never definitely major nor minor; they are constantly floating between the two, and the natural result is that they lack the vigour, the majesty, the sprightliness, the animation of our major mode; the plaintive sadness, the tender lamentations of our minor mode; and the charming effects resulting from the alternation of the two modes.

It is incontestable that Chinese music compares unfavourably with European music. From our point of view it certainly appears monotonous, even noisy—disagreeable, if you please; but what matters this if the Chinese themselves are satisfied with it? And that they are satisfied, that they like it, that it is a necessity for them, is fully proved by the constant use of music in their ceremonies and festivities; by the numerous bands parading the streets and offering their services; by the strict attention with which they listen to the ballad singers,—now exhibiting emotion at an affecting picture of suffering, now bursting into hearty laughter when the subject is of an amusing kind; and finally, by the large variety of instruments which, although often played without taste or feeling, are nevertheless remarkable for their beautiful simplicity of form, and their extreme cheapness. According to the Chinese themselves, music proceeds from the heart of man; it is the expression of the feelings of the heart.